Making Love
with Scripture

Making Love
with Scripture

WHY THE BIBLE DOESN'T MEAN
HOW YOU THINK IT MEANS

JACOB D. MYERS

Fortress Press

Minneapolis

MAKING LOVE WITH SCRIPTURE
Why the Bible Doesn't Mean What You Think It Means

Cover design: Brad Norr
Book design: PerfecType, Nashville, TN

Library of Congress Cataloging-in-Publication Data is available
Print ISBN: 978-1-4514-9955-1
eISBN: 978-1-5064-0260-4

The paper used in this publication meets the minimum requirements of American National Standard for Information Sciences — Permanence of Paper for Printed Library Materials, ANSI Z329.48-1984.

Manufactured in the U.S.A.

For Abby and Taylor

"Love never falters." (1 Cor. 13:8)

Contents

Acknowledgments ix

Introduction: Does the Dude *Really* Abide?
Making Theological Meaning 1

1. Shake 'n Bake: Reading Scripture with Ricky Bobby 13

Part I
Fifty Shades of Grey (Matter): Liberating God's Liberating Word / 29

2. How to Get Away with Murder: The Death
   of the Author 33

3. 99 Problems but the Text Ain't One:
   Cultural Interpretations of Scripture 43

4. Sméagol Knows the Way: Liberation Theologies
   of Scripture 57

Part II
Oppa Gangnam Style: The Bible as Rave / 71

5. Beware the Kragle: The World of Deconstruction 75

6. May the Odds Be Ever in Your Favor:
   The Hunger Games of (Biblical) Interpretation 85

7. Don't Win the Game. Change It:
   Radical Theologies of Scripture 97

Part III
This Is How We Do It:
Reading the Bible Today / 111

8. Selflessness and Bravery Aren't All That Different:
   The Self before the Wor(l)d 119

9. What Does the Fox Say? Listening to the Wor(l)d 133

10. You Can't Handle the Truth: The Saturated Wor(l)d . . . 145

Conclusion: Why Harry Potter Always Beats Voldemort:
The Power of Love 157

Notes 163

Acknowledgments

I would like to thank Will Bergkamp and the fine folks at Fortress Press for conceiving Theology for the People. I especially wish to thank Tony Jones for inviting me to contribute to this series and for guiding this project to completion, and Lisa Gruenisen, whose editorial kung fu is very strong. I also wish to express my appreciation for the folks at Homebrewed Christianity—its elders, deacons, and participants—for opening up new ways of engaging theology *for the people*.

Next, I would like to thank my friends Eric Barreto, Brennan Breed, Melissa Browning, Dave Garber, Tim Hartman, Mark Jefferson, Raj Nadella, and Nikki Young, who graciously and helpfully read early drafts of this book's chapters and/or shared invaluable insights that have made it all the better. Thanks also to Dave and Michelle Garber for their insightful guidance on Geek Culture. I also want to thank comedian and social critic John Oliver for showing me that cheekiness can also be smart and oriented toward justice.

Lastly, and most importantly, I want to thank Abby Myers, my best friend and life partner, and my amazing daughter Taylor, whose support and encouragement made this book possible. I love you beyond words, my perfect ladies.

Does the Dude *Really* Abide? Making Theological Meaning

Only those who struggle against evil by following the example
of the Crucified will
discover him at their side. To claim the comfort of the Crucified
while rejecting his way
is to advocate not only cheap grace but a deceitful ideology.
— MIROSLAV VOLF[1]

We make theological meaning the way we make love: with body, mind, heart, and soul. To do it otherwise is not to do it at all. Now, I know that love-making and Bible reading rarely share the same pillow, but maybe that's part of the problem. Perhaps that's one of the reasons why so few Westerners read the Bible anymore. It's time to spice things up. The world depends on it.

I hope you've seen the Coen brothers' 1998 film, *The Big Lebowski*. If not, just follow along like you have. In the film's final scene, the protagonist, Jeff Lebowski (aka the Dude), shares a few lines of dialogue with a character known to us only as the Stranger. The scene unfolds at the same bowling alley that stages much of the film.

"Take it easy, Dude. I know that you will," the Stranger says. The Dude replies with characteristic nonchalance: "Yeah. Well, the Dude abides." The Stranger then speaks to the camera. With a wry smile, the Stranger says, "The Dude abides. I don't know about you, but I take comfort in that. It's good knowin' he's out there. The Dude. Taking 'er easy for all us sinners." If your approach to biblical interpretation is at all like the Dude's approach to life, i.e., if no one's ever asked you to think critically about *how* you approach scripture, then this book is for you.

But here's the deal: No one, I repeat, *no one* merely abides, not even the Dude. Life, like biblical interpretation, doesn't just happen—not even for the dudeliest of white dudes.

The Dude's "taking 'er easy" way of being in the world is a foil for most of us, especially those of us who engage the Bible in search of a Word from the Lord.[2] Just like the Dude's narrative existence, Christian theologies of scripture and their concomitant interpretations arise out of conflicts. And yet, very much *unlike* the Dude, such theologies of scripture do not remain unaffected by cultural and philosophical change.

With the confidence of Burt Reynolds's mustache, European and Anglo-American white dudes have determined scriptural meaning according to what they/we (I am a white dude, after all) have predetermined as *neutral, objective,* and *universal.* Biblical meaning is purported to be *contextually blind.* Such a premise is grounded on a theological assumption.

If God is unchanging, immutable like the "unmoved mover" of Greek philosophy (thanks a lot, Aristotle), then is not the God at work in and through scripture radically unaffected by the ups and downs of human existence? Inasmuch as scripture *reveals* God to humankind, ought not the task of interpreting scripture be one of leading us beyond the text's cultural particularity to the absolute and universal teachings of a God who does not change?

Yeah, not so much; but historically this is what white dudes have argued.

From this theological assumption, so-called "mainstream" methods of biblical interpretation (read: Euro-American, heterosexual, affluent, male interpretations) arose as the "correct" way to interpret scripture.[3] The myth of the biblical scholar or theologian as the Dude, "taking 'er easy for all us sinners," must be dispelled—nay, we must drive a stake into its cold vampire heart. Why? Because it's literally sucking the life out of the church! #Buffy #Trueblood

The history of Christian theology teaches us nothing if it does not teach us this: *theologies are forged in the crucible of conflict.* Such conflict arises out of change, whether philosophical, political, or cultural. A colloquial way of putting this from my neck of the woods is that *if it ain't broke, don't fix it.* Our Bible reading is broken. Let's work together to fix it.

Pro tip: there is not, nor has there ever been, *one way* of reading scripture. All theologies of scripture are laden with ideological, political, and ethnic assumptions. We must recognize the ways in which *our* circumstances and prejudices shape our interpretations and theologies of scripture. Furthermore, because there is no one, absolute, and unalterable mode of interpretation, Christ-followers must develop the capacity to think critically about the ways in which our theologies are forged in the fires of our own contemporary conflicts and changes.

What Have You Gotten Yourself Into?

Taking nothing for granted, let's begin by defining *theology*. Way back in 1968, a Peruvian priest named Gustavo Gutiérrez wrote that if theology is nothing more than a treatise or discourse about God, then it really doesn't tell us much. He's right. This, by the way, is the classic, Western definition of theology. Such an understanding of theology masks much.

Father Gutiérrez continues by articulating a more helpful understanding of theology that participates in one's *lived experiences, attitudes,* and *commitment* to God.[4] In short, theology is an *inward* conviction that drives *outward* expression. Theology is something you freaking *do!*

How about a theology of *scripture?*

A theology of anything works to clarify our thinking about God as related to that particular something. A theology of the body, for instance, structures a certain understanding of the Divine in relation to human corporeality and how we treat, or fail to treat, bodies. #BlackLivesMatter Accordingly, a theology of scripture *seeks to articulate a person's lived experiences and concrete practices in relation to the Bible.* Remember this; it'll be on the test.

Okay, before we dive into the juicy parts, I'd like to let you in on what you've gotten yourself into. This book is prescriptive or, better, it is descriptive in route to being prescriptive. I make no pretense that I am neutral on the issues I describe—I'm quirky like that.

I don't believe in neutrality. Objectivity is a myth. But that doesn't mean I'm merely slingin' poo against the wall and hoping some of it will stick. This approach works if you work it. So, before I lure you in with my cheekiness, know that I'm going to tell you the truth as best as I understand it and urge you to lean into a certain way—my way—of being with scripture. Throughout, I make no attempts to conceal my convictions or temper my earnestness. This is an argument, and I want you to agree with me. #hollerifyouhearme

This book is not a choose-your-own-adventure. I want you to join me in *my* adventure with scripture, and I hope that you will enjoy the ride as much as I do. This book is not an all-you-can-eat salad bar, either. I don't lay out every conceivable option, inviting you to choose whatever tickles your fancy. The contemporary church and the theological academy are rife with such nonsense. Lastly, this is not a tell-all book. If you are looking for a book on the history of biblical interpretation or a comprehensive guide to contemporary biblical theologies, you'll need to look elsewhere. Sorry, the Apostle Paul may have tried to be all things to all people; but I'm not Paul, nor did Paul have to conform to modern publishing conventions.

Herein you'll find one dude's theology of scripture. To the degree that you find it helpful, it's yours. If it fails to resonate with your particular brand of theology, no worries! We can still be friends. Blog about it. What have I missed? Tweet it: #mlw/s. At what points do you disagree? The bottom line is this: we have enough of those mealy-mouthed tomes that use a butt-ton of words to say very little. Just think of this book as you would my car: it's still my car, but you are welcome to take it for a test drive (just bring it back with a full tank).

Jesus Wants You to Stop Masturbating

Okay, spoiler alert: this book will teach you how to make love with scripture. But, yeah, prepositions matter. If you were looking for a book to teach you how to make love *to* scripture—first off, *eww*, second off, WTF?—this is not the book for you. The title of this book is as parsimonious as it is playful. It means in (at least) two ways.

First, making love with scripture advances a relationship with the Bible that cuts across hundreds of years of scriptural engagement. In the period known as modernity—roughly from René Descartes (b. 1596) onward—people have been taught to think in a particular way. Descartes's adage, *I think, therefore I am* (*cogito, ergo sum*), conditions us to think of ourselves in a certain way. At the same time, it leads us to think of everything and everyone that is *not* us in a totally different way. Let's break this down like a fraction.

Descartes wanted to establish a way for people (read: white dudes) to know the things that they know with absolute *certainty*. Thus, he started to doubt everything—his thoughts, his senses, his dreams. At last he came to the conclusion that he could doubt everything except for the fact that he was the one doing the doubting. He could not deny that he was a "thinking thing" (a *res cogitans*, in case you want to impress your friends with some Latin at the next pub-crawl: "Kiss my *res cogitans*, Leroy!" Umm, no. Ahem.). By doing this, Descartes established the primacy of the solitary, thinking individual as the starting point for all knowledge, driving a wedge between human subjects and the objects of our experience.

But here's the problem. The God who reveals Godself in and through scripture is not a *thing* that we can understand all by our lonesome. Nor is the world God loves a thing. You can't approach scripture the way you approach a trilobite fossil; you can't study it the way you study DNA. Pay attention now because this is the thesis of this book: *The only way to approach the Word of God revealed in and through scripture is by making love with it.* #allyouneedislove

If you have kids, think about how you know them. By first loving them, you are able to know them in a way that their teachers or pediatrician cannot. It does not mean that your child's teacher or doctor does not possess genuine knowledge of her; it's just that they know your child *differently* than you do.

The erotic approach, which I'll explain later, helps us to yearn for God's life-giving, liberating Word revealed in and through scripture. This doesn't mean that much of what you read in scholarly biblical commentaries is worthless. It's just a different kind of knowledge. Love does not lock rational thought in the brig; but it doesn't let it steer the ship, either.

Philology (the historical study of literary texts and languages) and archeology are not theology. This does not mean that they aren't important fields of inquiry. A pediatrician's way of knowing your child is necessary to monitor his health, after all. What I want to stress is that the way many biblical scholars and theologians study scripture—through techniques that make up the meat-and-potatoes of most seminary teaching on the Bible, by the way—has very little to do with the God who lovingly counts the hairs on our heads. But you already knew this, didn't you?

I don't believe that you *can* know God apart from love.[5] This is one reason why so-called "objectivity" has no business with things divine. You cannot know God objectively because God is forever beyond objectification. So, if you want to encounter God through Holy Scripture you must be willing to make *love* with scripture, that is, *to make love happen in yourself and in the world through your engagement with scripture.*

Second, making love with scripture means that the Bible is not just about you and your special Jesus friend. *grabs guitar, dons Snuggy, sings "The More I Seek You"* This Jesus-is-my-boyfriend theology must be abolished in the face of the real suffering and real injustice in our world. In other words, the Bible intends to get you off your ass and out into the world to *make* love and peace happen in a world suffused with evil and pain. God wants you to *participate* in God's mission, dammit—a mission to make all things new in Christ Jesus! Did ya think that when Jesus said, "If any of you wants to be my follower, you must turn from your selfish ways, take up your cross daily, and follow me" (Luke 9:23) he was being facetious? I see no winky-face emoticon in my version of the Bible. Scripture *becomes* Holy Scripture only when it drives us to a *holy* way of being in the world, a way that is *wholly* for human and non-human others.

Such a way of being is beyond ethical and political quietism. We must not accept the status quo when so many are in pain and calling for justice. The difference between scripture as a collection of warm 'n fuzzy aphorisms for personal enlightenment or self-actualization and scripture as an impetus driving us to participate in God's mission in the world is the difference between masturbation and procreation.

If you find yourself masturbating with scripture, stop it! Seriously! There are people here.

Making love with scripture is action-oriented. It's procreative. Father Gutiérrez is right: any theology worthy of the name is something you *do* with and for others. You cannot do it by yourself. This is why God has grafted us into the beloved community called the church.

Okay, enough with masturbation. Let's talk about the subtitle.

The subtitle of this book riffs off of a recurring line from *The Princess Bride*. #RIPAndré Throughout the film, the Sicilian boss Vizzini repeatedly uses the word "inconceivable," almost like it's an expletive. At one point, Vizzini's Spanish swordsman, Inigo Montoya, remarks, "How come you keep using that word? I do not think it means what you think it means."

I have intentionally adapted this phrase to help us move beyond our modern obsession with connecting the Bible and *meaning*. The Bible is irreducible to its intellectual content. It transcends knowledge. Its meaningfulness means *more* than the meanings we assign to it. This is one of the things that separates it from any other work of literature. As the African Bishop St. Augustine (354–430 CE) maintained, even the most penetrating mind can only scratch the surface of the text's significance.[6] All this is to say that *how* the Bible means is different from both *what* it means and the ways in which other texts mean.

The Bible does not exist simply to contribute to your aesthetic joy or to enhance your knowledge of things divine. It does do these things, but that is not its primary purpose. Herein lies my theological claim regarding Holy Scripture—wait for it: *the Bible exists to shape your way of being in the world with God and creation*. Thus, understanding *what* scripture means is not the same thing as understanding *how* it means.

What's at Stake for Us Theologically in Biblical Interpretation?

Even as theologies of scripture have often been conflated with ways of interpreting scripture, they are not the same thing. It's a bit like the old chicken-and-egg causality dilemma: Which comes first, our understanding of how to interpret scripture by which we learn about God, or our understanding of God revealed in scripture by which we learn how to interpret scripture? You can see how this question is as convoluted as a drunken game of Twister.

Here's the dealeo: our so-called "age of intelligence" actually blocks us from thinking intelligently about our own intelligence. Especially in regard to our theologies. Western ways of knowing create a kind of blindness; they prevent us from seeing what God is up to in and through scripture.[7] Mainstream interpretive strategies that claim to offer us a clearer view of biblical meaning can actually block us from seeing anything new and life-giving in scripture. The ways we learn to interpret scripture determine in advance what we will find in it.

To illustrate, the situation of most Western Christ-followers is a bit like the milieu created by James Dashner in his novel, *The Maze Runner*. In that novel, a group of adolescent boys is sequestered to a grassy area called the Glade. The Glade is surrounded by a colossal maze that simultaneously situates their bondage and the promise of their release. Such is the nature of a maze. Some of the boys have been trapped in the Glade for years, but the story begins when Thomas, the story's protagonist, enters the Glade for the first time.

You see, the boys have always selected the fastest among them to serve as runners. It's their job to venture daily into the maze in search of a way out. Such foreknowledge about a maze conditions the boys' approach to the maze. A maze exists for us to find our way through it. Right? That's its purpose, or so the boys imagine.

In a pivotal scene in the story, Thomas realizes that the maze is nothing but a ruse designed to test them. As the story unfolds,

Thomas's observation proves correct. The purpose of the maze in *The Maze Runner* is not to complicate the boys' escape; rather, the purpose is to see how long they will persevere when the possibility of escape has been removed.

For many of us, our approach to scripture has centered on discerning the one, true meaning of the text and to strive to live into that truth in our lives. What if I told you that scripture is a maze with no exit, a labyrinth that lures us in only to never let us go? What would you say if I told you that the purpose of scripture is to keep us running, searching, striving—to catalyze our desire to love God and neighbor? Would you kick off your Asics in disgust? Or would you begin to see your forays into the biblical maze in a different light?

Theologies of Scripture: A Thru-Hiker's Guide

As I mentioned above, Holy Scripture and theology relate to one another like a chicken and an egg. Even if it's undecidable which came first, there is no doubt that they exist in a causal relationship. Chickens lay eggs, which break open into chickens. Duh! Likewise, one's theology of scripture *breaks open* the text in certain ways, and interpretation is the term for just such a breaking. Interpretations give birth to particular theologies. Such is a theology of scripture.

I don't want to overcook this metaphor—Oh no you didn't! Yes! Yes, I did!—I do, however, want to make the following claim: the only wrong way to adjudicate the chicken-egg relationship is to deny that the relationship exists. If your theology ignores the role interpretation plays in it, you are wrong. Likewise, the only incorrect way to interpret scripture is to fail to attend to the theological, cultural, and philosophical connections that flow from it and undergird it. #nuffsaid!

Of course, this argument is based on *my* interpretation, *my* theology of scripture. It is logically fallacious to argue that there are no absolutes, except for my declaration against absolutes.

Absolutely! At day's end, the theology of scripture you are now reading is just as contingent upon *my* cultural, philosophical, and theological assumptions as every other. I leave it for you to decide if you're gonna smoke what I'm rolling. #puffpuffpass

Excursus: Dear White People

Let me go ahead and slow this track way down so you can really hear what I'm saying. There is no such thing as a *true* or *right* interpretation of scripture. That does not mean that there are no *wrong* interpretations. All it means is that every act of interpretation is contextually situated. Every act of interpretation is always already structured by certain ethnic, political, ideological, and theological commitments. This shouldn't frighten us; rather, it ought to drive us to think deeply about how our individual and communal acts of interpretation might participate in ways of thinking that work against what we believe ourselves to profess theologically.

Where biblical interpretations are concerned, everything comes into play and nothing can be ignored. Gender, race, sexual orientation, education, class, political affiliation, all-time highest Space Invaders score—*everything* shapes the kinds of questions we ask of scripture. The kinds of questions we ask *of* the Bible structure the kinds of answers we receive *from* it. There is no view from nowhere—and this assertion, too, is a view from *somewhere*. We cannot ignore how our existence and ways of knowing take form out of the weave and weft of cosmic chaos.

Here's my *from somewhere*: I'm a white, mostly straight, well-educated, middle-class, American, cisgender man (and cisgender means that my gender identity—male—matches the one assigned to me at birth—Hi, Mom!). By right of birth and social conditioning, I have learned to interpret the Bible in particular ways. At no point am I able to set aside these features. They abide in my very flesh, simultaneously forming my viewpoint and blocking my access to other points of view.

That's why I read the work of others who don't share my characteristics. It's important, y'all! It's all that stands between us and the coming (and entirely-made-up) Churchpocalypse.

Just as no person or community has unimpeded access to God, there has never been a path to biblical interpretation that ain't messy as bathroom buckshot. Repeat after me: *theologies of scripture don't just happen.* You can't do a little ballerina twirl and expect theological meaning to drop out of the sky.

So, rather than doubling-down on theologies of scripture that substantiate the reigning power structures—structures that favor white supremacy and male privilege—or abandoning scripture as a vestige of oppression, what if we let the Spirit do her work on us? That's what the rest of this book is about: opening us up to the life-giving, world affirming Word of God. By this we just might find the power to make the world a better place. You with me? *Freeze-frame high five* Too soon? Okay.

For starters, let's go ahead and agree to dispel the myth, which is perpetuated by all sorts of readings, that we white dudes can saunter up to the Word of God in our bathrobes, White-Russian in hand, and render a universal, absolute interpretation before breakfast. We must consider how our "taking 'er easy" theologies and Dude-ly ways of interpreting scripture foster the oppression and marginalization of others. Making love begins where objectification ends.

Chapter One

Shake 'n Bake:
Reading Scripture
with Ricky Bobby

Because reality is always in process, the meaning and the
*   impact of concepts in reality change*
through time and space. . . . Similarly, theology is influenced by
*   the ideological and material grounds*
of the historical reality from which it emerges.
— MAYRA RIVERA[1]

Fact: *Talladega Nights: The Ballad of Ricky Bobby* is one of the funniest films of all time. #shakenbake Maybe it's because of the many years I've lived in the southeastern United States, or maybe it's on account of my juvenile sense of humor, or maybe because I hold all things NASCAR in rather low esteem (seriously, they just drive in circles for hours on end)—perhaps all three—but I am not ashamed to admit that I can quote most of this film verbatim.

One of the funniest scenes in the movie is centered on prayer.

With his family and best friend and racing partner Cal Naughton Jr. gathered around the supper table, eager to enjoy the bountiful harvest of Domino's Pizza, KFC, and "the always delicious Taco Bell," Ricky Bobby leads his family in saying grace.

Ricky Bobby's prayer is remarkable in many ways, but the most theologically significant aspect of his prayer is that it's directed exclusively toward *Baby* Jesus. When his wife Carley interrupts his prayer in frustration that Ricky always prays to Baby Jesus, he replies, "Well, look, I'm saying grace and I like the Christmas Jesus best. When you say grace you can say it to Grownup Jesus, or Teenage Jesus, or Bearded Jesus, or whoever you want."

Here's the point of this brief excursion into cinematic awesomeness: We worship the God we know. For Christ-followers, the Bible shapes our conception of God, but how we understand the God revealed in and through scripture is in turn shaped by our contexts. Perhaps this is not done as overtly as it is for Ricky Bobby and his family members, but we too do this.

The Great Disturbance: Love Meets Life

Interpreting scripture shapes theologies of scripture, which shape interpretations of scripture. Around and around we go on the merry-go-round of faith. Trying to arrest the movement of God in and through scripture is like trying to draw a bird in flight—kind of hard to do unless you are Bob Ross, and he's got that luscious Afro full of super powers to help him.[2] #happyclouds

Here's another thing. No one has ever made biblical meaning in a vacuum. We can do nothing in a vacuum—including vacuum. True story. We see this clearly in Acts chapter 8 when Philip encounters a financial officer in the service of the Queen of Ethiopia. Philip asks the man, "Do you really understand what you are reading?" To which the man replies famously, "How can I without someone to guide me?" Understanding takes place in community,

especially biblical understanding. Discerning the meaning of biblical texts is like locating dwarven doors in Tolkien's Middle Earth:
both must be viewed in the proper light. The doors to scriptural
meaning are utterly invisible to those without the proper angle of
vision—a community-shaped vision.[3]

Just as the Ethiopian official came to understand scripture
through Philip's guidance, I too have come to regard scripture
by a certain light. This framework for understanding scripture
is drawn from Jesus' assertion that the greatest commandment is
to love God with all that you are and to love your neighbor as
yourself (Matt. 22:37-40). My own faith formation and theological training have led me to the following belief: *The Bible exists to
open us intellectually, emotionally, and bodily toward others—Divine,
human, and nonhuman. Such radical openness toward others the
Bible calls "love."* This theological wager shapes how I understand
the Bible and how I try to treat others. I think it's a pretty good
place to begin.

Yeah! Love! Everybody loves 'em some love, right? But here's
the problem: the concept of love is as thick and snarled as a 1970s
pubic tangle—and I ain't hatin'. Keep it real, Fleetwood Mac! Ain't
no shame in your game! Because of love's innate complexity we are
going to need to think through what we even mean by love before
we can begin to employ love as a framework for understanding
where we stand in relation to Holy Scripture.

Love is both utterly simple and infinitely complex. Our everyday speech bears witness to this tension. We talk about *falling* in
love, as if it were a force that takes hold of us like gravity. At the
same time, if you asked ten people to define love, after the stutter-
ing and stammering ceased you would likely receive ten different
answers. How can love be both universal and particular? Love is
one of those things that's difficult to talk about, but we know it
when we see it. As one thinker puts it, "We live with love as if we
knew what it was about. But as soon as we try to define it, or at
least approach it with concepts it draws away from us."[4] My own

experiences with love affirm the truth of this assessment. How 'bout yours?

God Is Love: Learning from Scripture

Scripture itself, and 1 John 4 in particular, guides my thinking toward what I will come to call an *erotic theology of scripture*: an approach to God in and through scripture that is guided by love. (Btw, my use of the word "erotic" is not reducible to sensuality, but I'll say more about that later.)

If love is to be more than a gesture of theological hand waving, a bit of interpretive hocus-pocus, then we need at least a cursory understanding of what we mean by love before we proceed. Love is an easy concept to equivocate, and if we're not careful we will reason from our mundane understanding of love toward God's understanding of love. On account of this proclivity, we must bracket what we think we know about love and allow the love we're talking about to conform to God's definition of love revealed in the Bible.

The writer of 1 John urges us to love one another *because* "love is from God" (4:7). Okay, so for starters we learn that love emerges *out of* God. The outward directionality is more pronounced in the Greek. At the same time, in the same verse, love draws us *into* God and such in-drawing is the means by which we are *able* to know God.[5] Thus, love as a force in the world is both centrifugal and centripetal; it flows out of God *and* draws us into God.

Without pausing for a breath, the writer of 1 John declares that "God is love" (v. 8). The love of which the writer speaks is not an adjective, but a noun. He (or she—we don't know who wrote 1 John) isn't saying that God is *loving, lovely,* or *lovable.* God *is* love. Love both defines God and defines love. Moreover, we don't know what love *is* until we see it among us in the sending of God's only begotten son into the world "so that we might live *through* him" (v. 9). Hmm.

Moving on, in verse 10, the writer of 1 John makes sure we don't get this whole thing bass-ackwards: it's not by *our* understanding of love that we come to understand both love and God; but it is by *God's* self-revelation of Godself *as love* that we come to know both. Just like a shotgun, the direction you point the thing makes all the difference.

Love, redefined for us by God's outpouring of Godself, enables us to abide *in God* (vv. 12-13). This is a spatial construction. Loving the world in the way modeled by Jesus *causes* us to dwell in God. It's not that God *is* creation, nor that God is life in a simplistic sense, as certain theologies suggest; rather, in love all of life is *drawn into* God even as God's love *flows into* life.[6] God-is-love is not static. Loving in this way enables us to breathe the very breath of God (v. 13; cf. John 20:22, where Jesus breathes on his disciples), which is . . . wait for it . . . love.

In verses 16-17, we read again that God is love and that inasmuch as we abide in love we abide in God. By this, both love and we who abide in love are made perfect. That is, "we are exactly the same as God is in this world." Love overcomes our imperfection, making us like God and able to approach the world and all that is within it out of love rather than fear (v. 18).

One final word of commentary before we proceed. In 1 John 4:19 we read, "We love because God first loved us." This reiterates what the writer of 1 John has been trying to tell us all along: we don't fully understand love until God shows us what it is, and through it, who God is for us in the person of Jesus Christ. Such love makes the distinction between a spiritual love of God and a sociopolitical love of others forever untenable. Spirituality and liberation are one.[7] Therefore, love begins with a kind of double-vision, one that sees the Word of God revealed *in* and *through* scripture, and that sees the self in relation to the other with the eyes of love.

Love Is from God: Living in and through Scripture

If love comes from God even as it draws us into God, then it stands to reason that God's radical outpouring and in-drawing will change us in some fundamental way. The writer of 1 John does not say,

"Y'all just keep on doin' what yur doin', aight!" as he spits tobacco into an empty Bud Light can. No. God calls us toward a perfection guided by love of God and neighbor. Unfortunately, just like our ole pal Ricky Bobby, we are rooted in our respective cultures; they already shape how we see the world, including the world of the biblical text. In order to orient ourselves toward love, we need to get a better understanding of the roadblocks and pitfalls to love arising out of our cultural contexts and attitudes.

The nature of the writerly-readerly relationship between you and me means that I can't address *your* cultural context because a) I don't know who you are or where you come from, and b) even if I did know you, I wouldn't have access to all of the experiences in your life that make you see the world as you do. You are in a better position to critique your own contextually conditioned ways of knowing than anyone. I can assume, however, that if you're reading this book you can read English, which means you were born into or have acculturated yourself to a Western way of thinking. Language and rationality are entwined, didn't ya know?

I am ambivalent about Western Christianity in the twenty-first century. It has formed me to see the world in particular ways, but not all of those ways are conducive to my efforts to follow God in the way of Jesus. I feel the same way about Western Christianity that I do about every song ever sung by Toby Keith—kind of proud to be an American, but also kind of guilty that we are the world's biggest assholes. I choose Christ over Uncle Sam; but even this choice is shaped by a culture that has led me to believe I can make such a choice, which isn't universal.

Theology, how we understand God and participate in God's mission in the world, is the love-child of life and scripture. Both are essential. The problem of theology is that Western Christianity is far more Western than it is Christian. *Theology* is not even a Christian word. It's a loanword from Western philosophy. The word appears nowhere in the Bible and it is highly unlikely that Jesus would've ever spoken in such terms. Coined by Plato, the term *theology* was later adopted by Aristotle to differentiate the myths about the gods from philosophy proper.[8] So, when we who are Westerners move toward a theology of scripture that is guided by love, we have to do a bit of ground clearing to keep the weeds of Western thought from choking the life out of our erotic flora.

There are three marks of love that we need to disentangle from Western thought. Think of these as the three essential ingredients in any erotic brew: the self, the other, and the distance between them. Let's look at each of these in turn.

The Self beyond Certainty

Are you sitting down? Good, you shouldn't be walking and reading—you could fall into a Smurf snare and Gargamel will catch you and feed you to his cat. Ahem. Okay, here it is: the self does not exist. *Kabloom!* Just blew your mind, didn't I? I told you to sit down. The self is a product of Western thought that has no independent existence apart from the processes by which it is made.[9] Allow me to explain.

The modern notion of the self arose in tandem with the Enlightenment. The formation of the self as a fixed and independent entity in the world was a process. Many agree, however, that the self became the gravitational center around which the rest of the universe revolved—particularly following the philosophical advances made by René Descartes. His famous *I think, therefore I am* didn't just establish thought as the dominant form of expression; Descartes also invented the modern notion of the self by setting it in opposition to everything else.

Think of the pre-Cartesian self as a young Han Solo. He's handling his business on the Millennium Falcon with his co-pilot Chewbacca, full of his own comings and goings. One day he is captured by Boba Fet and, oh noes, he's sealed in carbonite to be delivered to Jabba the Hutt. In other words, the pre-Enlightenment self was not set; it was not a *fixed* point of reference until Descartes came along and set the self in opposition to everything else outside the mind.

Of course I am simplifying all of this, but there is no questioning the fact that Descartes established the self as a *subject*: a seemingly self-supported, unshakeable foundation of truth capable of achieving self-certainty. This certainty of the self's existence came at a price. In order to be certain of something, to know it beyond doubt, it cannot be free to change. If something has the ability to change, how can I ever keep up with it? Furthermore, if I can't keep up with something how can I really *know* it? This is the modern dilemma of the self that frustrates love.

In Western thought following Descartes, the self impedes love because the modern self exists to seize possession of the other, transforming everything beyond the self into an *object* of experience. You cannot love an object. You can only love an *other*. You don't really *love* pizza or going to Six Flags. You *enjoy* those things. They give you a certain degree of pleasure. The kind of love the Bible teaches us, and teaches us most clearly through the life and ministry of Jesus, is that love and certitude are mutually exclusive. Genuine knowledge of the world and all that is in it demands a different approach than the self who only knows according to certainty. To know an object is not the same thing as knowing a subject, and that's what we've got to learn to do if we want to love God and neighbor according to Jesus' teachings.

The Bible presents a different understanding of the self. Through scripture God teaches us that we are not what we know, but who knows us. We are not ourselves the foundation of truth, but anything worthy of the name truth is founded in God's self-revelation. We are not defined by what we have; rather, we are defined by who has us.

The Other beyond Certainty

The idea of an *other* beyond the self is not new. "No group ever defines itself as One without immediately setting up the Other opposite itself."[10] Greeks defined themselves in opposition to

Barbarians. Israelites to Philistines. Men to women. Whites to blacks. Jedi to Siths. Pure-bloods to Mud-bloods. This is so evident in history and pervasive across cultures that it's hardly worthy of mention, *but* (and this is a big but) scripture calls us to a different way of being in the world, a way beyond objectification.

In a fundamental sense, the other is necessary for the self as a subject. The sense of identity and even certainty that the self takes from the other is folded out of the differences between the self and the other. The other is defined by a certain *difference* (racially, ethnically, sexually, etc.), and this difference is then projected back onto the other as a lack, a deficiency, a cause for derision. Infamously, Sigmund Freud defined women not by what they have, but by what he perceived them to lack. Women lack penises; therefore, Freud reasoned, this lack of a penis is constitutive of woman's essential makeup. Pro tip: Few female-identified women walk around bemoaning their lack of a penis; many more bemoan Freud's lack of insight into "what women want."

Moving toward the other beyond objectification is not only frustrated by our perceived differences. Language itself betrays the other. Every utterance about another reduces the other to the parameters established by the one doing the uttering (i.e., the self). In other words, when I write a sentence in English—in any Western language—I must announce a subject who performs some action, and such an action is often directed to an object (e.g., "Dick sees Jane."). The subject does the acting. The object receives the action. Active/passive. Giver/receiver. A certain duality is already in operation here at our most basic level of thought.

The Hebrew language too structures thought in such a way. However, I believe we can learn much from the fact that the Israelites, along with Jews who adhere to this theological tradition, do not pronounce the name of God. This simple gesture of reverence, of awe at a linguistic level, recognizes that we tilt toward objectification, toward idolatry. Devout Jews teach us how language itself can be used as a kind of offering to God. They regard God's name as holy: set apart, beyond certainty.

I use the nebulous term "other" on purpose. Its lack of specificity is a good thing, at least for the purposes of this book, because it is less objectifying than its synonyms. Taking a page from the Hebrew playbook, I employ the term "other" to apply to human others and God-as-other, but the term ought also be employed toward nonhuman others. Rainforests, animals, watersheds, mountaintops, ecosystems, and so on are also *other* than the self. They too can be reduced to mere things to be exploited for economic gain, or they can be regarded lovingly, as inherently worthy of preservation and protection.

As soon as we move in the direction of loving the other beyond objectification we must admit that the Bible too is guilty of such objectification. John speaks of "the Jews" in his Gospel as if the mere mention of them is an expletive. Gentiles. Gays. Women. Slaves. The Bible doesn't get a bye from slipping into prejudicial and pejorative descriptions of the other much like Bill Murray doesn't get a bye from being awesome. The presence of such objectification in scripture is proof of one of two things: Either God shares our proclivity to fear, mistrust, and even hate others, or God is so eager to enter into relationship with us that God is willing to risk God's own reputation by allowing Godself to be thought. I'm putting my chips on the latter.

It's easier to accept this second option when you realize that there is a counter-testimony also present in scripture, one that challenges objectification and xenophobia. Consider the final verses in the book of Jonah. The whole book is saturated with Jonah's ethnic disdain for the wealthy Ninevites. Jonah literally runs in the opposite direction when God calls him to preach to them and ends up in the belly of a large fish. And then, when he finally preaches God's message of repentance, the Ninevites do exactly what Jonah told them to do: they repent and turn to God. Jonah shows his undies by his response. God's reaction to Jonah constitutes the only instance where a book of the Bible ends with a question. God asks, in effect, "What do you care if I show compassion to the Ninevites?" Damn, God even cares about the one-percenters! #whodathunkit?

The Bible offers another way of approaching the other, not as a stranger to be feared, but as a neighbor to be embraced. To illustrate, think of that scene in *The Fellowship of the Ring* where Gandalf faces off with Balrog (the shadow demon brandishing a flaming whip and sword) on the Bridge of Khazad-dûm. Gandalf summons a shield and cries, "You shall not pass!" That's kind of what the love of God and neighbor demands. Love casts a hedge of protection around the other, barring unfettered access to the other. Love calls us beyond objectification.

The Distance beyond Disclosure

The final necessary element in love is the distance created and maintained between the self and the other, between the lover and her beloved. This distance is crucial. And it is precisely this distance that is disclosed upon and collapses under the weight of Western ways of thinking. Objectification eradicates distance. Objectification operates like Pac-Man, gobbling up others only to be haunted by the ghost of the other whose only recourse is to withdraw.

Western thought, as I've already mentioned, is oriented toward *objective* knowledge. It wants to reduce everything that the self encounters to an *object* of experience. This act of radical reduction, where the other is demoted to the rank of an object, erases the distance between the self and the other.

Love demands that we *keep* our distance, that we not muddy the other's carpet with our dirty-ass intellectual sneakers. This becomes a bit easier as we come to respect the fact that a certain spacing between the self and the other is necessary.

For example, if there were no distance whatsoever between my spouse and me, how could we be in relationship? It is precisely because of the distance between us that we are able to love each other, and this distance that prevails between us does double duty in love.

On the one hand, the distance between us creates the possibility for yearning. Distance makes desire possible. The distance between us does something to me. It is active. Distance allows a sense of longing to stir up inside me—a hunger to know her more fully, to know her to the fullest extent. The distance allows me to draw toward her as if pulled in by an emotional tractor beam. Our twenty years of intimacy are preserved precisely because neither of us has disclosed fully upon the other.

Sure, there are things that I can tell you objectively about my wife. She has green eyes, for instance. But then, as soon as I utter those words, the second they escape my lips, they seem to fall short. The color green cannot capture the many shades of color, the multiple ways of meaning, the countless hours of engagement signified by such an objective statement as "she has green eyes." My wife is irreducible to her bodily features. Sure, to *you* she's a lady with green eyes; to me, those green eyes signal so much more— they structure my very existence.

On the other hand, the distance between us is a kind of pact. Even as it draws me close, it bars my access. The otherness of the other cannot be taken; it can only be received. Love heeds the look of the other as a command: Thou shall not kill. Of course, millions who have been objectified—used and abused to satisfy the insatiable appetites of people with more power—know that objectification is a kind of murder. Objectification can be worse than death.

History bears witness to this. The "final solution" was only possible after the Nazis turned the Jews, along with countless others, into *objects*. Only objects can be discarded. To kill the other you must first objectify the other; that's why I think Jesus told his disciples not to reduce the other to the rank of "idiot" or "fool" because such objectification makes murder possible (Matt. 5:21-6). We see this so clearly today in the marginalization of those with mental illness, who can be dismissed and discarded. Even the current vitriol in the U.S. between republicans and democrats displays the pernicious effects of objectification.

Distance is like topsoil. When it is abundant, life flourishes; but when it is not protected, life itself begins to erode. The Bible has names for this space that exists between the self and the other. It's called eternal or abundant life. Eternal life is only possible when the space between God and the self is preserved in love. Abundant life is only possible when the space between the self and others is maintained by love. This prompts two points of concern.

First, God's Word revealed *in* scripture must be allowed to keep its distance. When the Word of God in scripture is reduced to the mere semantic value of the words of the text, when this distance is not respected, the result is idolatry. The doctrine of biblical inerrancy, which forces the Word of God to conform to human ways of meaning, is a form of idolatry. It radically reduces God to a set of ideological assumptions projected in the name of God.

Love frees us from the temptation of such idolatry because it doesn't want to collapse the distance between the self and the Word. The Word "is" wholly other.[11] Even as the Word is powerful beyond thought or measure, it is revealed in the frailty of human language and culture. Making love with scripture will free you from idolatry. It will draw you more fully into God while at the same time holding you back from the human propensity to objectification, which is a form of violence.

Second, God's World revealed *through* scripture also requires distance (I say more about the World of God in part 3). The World revealed through scripture offers a particular way of seeing the cosmos—the World of the other. The Word structures our imagination, making possible a way of seeing the World according to God's hope and mission to "make all things new" (Rev. 21:5). When the distance that God's Wor(l)d produces in the world is not respected, the Bible can be wielded as a tool of oppression. We need look no farther than the modern missionary movement and its biblical justification of colonial oppression to see what happens when distance is disclosed upon.[12]

God's World revealed through scripture yields love. It plants seeds of love that can structure an entirely different way of knowing, being, and acting in the world if we will let it. Through scripture we are able to discern the call of the other that says, "Don't kill me; love me." The World of God revealed through scripture structures a way of being that is radically *for* the other just as God is radically *for* creation in Jesus Christ. Distance is thus the proof that I have not reduced the other to an object of my experience. Just as the presence of hunger proves you are not full, the fact that the other's full identity is always in doubt tells me that I have not disclosed upon her subjectivity. Distance is counterintuitive. The drink becomes a thirst. The more I taste the bounty given to me by the other, the hungrier I grow.

Be the Change the Bible Wants You to Be

In those immortal words from the world's most eloquent orator (of course I'm talking about Rocky Balboa), we come to understand our charge as Christ-followers. Rocky cries, "If I can change, and you can change, then anybody can change." Wow! *grabs hanky* Sheer poetry.

Another prophet at another time said much the same thing. The Apostle Paul writes to the Christ-followers gathered at Philippi, "Make your thoughts, feelings, and attitudes toward others be like those which were also in Christ Jesus" (2:5), and to those gathered at Rome Paul says, "Don't allow yourselves to be conformed to the ways of being in this age, but allow yourselves to be transformed by the renewing of your minds" (12:2). This, at base, is the task of this book.

We require the means to swim against the current of Western Christianity. To love God and neighbors requires us to place our ways of thinking at risk by opening ourselves to the other in love. For such a transformation to take place in us we will have to find new ways of thinking and new ways of listening to God's Word revealed in and through scripture. Following Jesus' call to love both God and neighbor entails that we conform our thoughts and behaviors to the way of Jesus, the way of love.

Love of God and neighbor, though inextricable, must be treated separately because all too often in our current modes of thinking, being, and doing, both forms of love end up as self-love, perpetuating the Western patterns of objectification and marginalization.

Loving one's neighbor entails a certain listening for life empowered and structured by love. Such a listening arising *through* scripture demands that we listen to those voices that have been marginalized by Western modernity, and especially those on the underside of our current global economic structures. Listening to God's Word revealed through scripture opens us to love of the other as neighbor only when we refuse to turn from the neighbor's cries of injustice. Such love that the Wor(l)d requires of we who would follow Jesus means that we will attend to the ways in which other communities discern God's life-giving Word in their particular context.

God summons us to a different way of being with God and neighbor than we have grown accustomed to in modern Christianity. The erotic approach is the only way I can see to know God in and through scripture beyond objectification. The erotic approach will thus, by necessity, attend to *both* scripture *and* to human and nonhuman others in relation to the self. "Whoever loves God must also love others" (1 John 4:21). By the erotic approach, defined according to God's radical outpouring of Godself in Jesus, we can no longer separate God's self-revelation as *either* being in the Bible *or* in the world. Through scripture we discover God's love of the world even as we are admitted into God's mission for the world. This way of being with and in God subsumes all of creation; therefore, the erotic approach to God will always be *in* and *beyond* acts of biblical interpretation.

{ Part I }

Fifty Shades of Grey (Matter): Liberating God's Liberating Word

The Bible can be used as an instrument of domination,
but it can also be interpreted to work for our liberation.
— KWOK PUI-LAN[1]

Love requires listening. You cannot claim to love either God or
neighbor and shut your ears to the cries of injustice. Part I of this
book offers a way of listening to the cries of the oppressed and
marginalized in and through scripture. Because God has shown
us through scripture, and most clearly through Jesus, that love is
inherently life-affirming and oriented to human flourishing, we
must find ways of participating in love and life in and through

scripture. In this regard, *Fifty Shades of Grey* structures a helpful, if unlikely, metaphor.

You don't have to have read the book or watched the film *Fifty Shades of Grey* to know what it's about. And over 100 million people have purchased the book, so in spite of its abysmal reviews by critics, it has tugged something—stop it, *you* went there, not me—in the public imagination.[2]

From SNL skits to talk radio show punchlines, and a never-ending stream of puns by Jimmy Fallon on *The Tonight Show*, this story of a sexually and psychologically frustrated business magnate who seduces a naïve college student showcases the allure of sexual taboo and the nature of power. The narrative unfolds as the wealthy and handsome Christian Grey lures the young Anastasia Steele (seriously?) into his lurid fetishistic world of bondage/discipline and sadism/masochism (BDSM).

I bring up *Fifty Shades* to draw your attention to a much more serious matter. BDSM structures a relationship between persons similar to that of Western thought: by establishing opposites. This has been the case since Plato—er, it's hard to imagine Plato in the context of BDSM, but, yep, just did, and so did you. Crap! I feel violated. *shakes head vigorously*

Okay, so back to what I was saying. Western thought is like BDSM in that both depend on establishing opposites. White is set in opposition to black. Male is taken to be the opposite of female. And the list continues, to infinity and beyond! (man/woman, slave/free, Jew/Gentile, Greek/Barbarian, speech/writing, presence/absence, honey badger/all other animals that are not honey badgers, etc.). *Fifty Shades* displays the noxious effects of such hierarchical relationships: the intentional subordination and domination of the one to establish the authority and dominance of the other.

The history of biblical interpretation participates in something like the BDSM exhibited in *Fifty Shades*. We are not talking about sexual bondage and domination—although let us never forget that people have employed scripture to justify the rape and sexual humiliation of persons of color, women, and LGBTI (Lesbian, Gay, Bisexual, Transgender, Intersex) persons. There are (at least) two kinds of bondage in theologies of scripture: demographic bondage and intellectual bondage. These are not mutually exclusive; if the former applies it always includes the latter.

The history of Western Christianity is a history of demographic and intellectual BDSM.

I am told that BDSM relationships are structured like a contract. Boundaries are set, safe words are established, and roles are assumed by *willing* participants; in fact, the lack of such boundaries was one of the central criticisms of *Fifty Shades*. And rightly so. There is no pleasure for the subordinated/dominated person in demographic and intellectual domination. Nor is the pain inflicted upon those on the underside of power structures undertaken by willing consent. BDSM without consent is rape.

There is a second reason why I mention *Fifty Shades of Grey*—*grey*, if you're British, and *gray*, if you're American (te'mātō/te'mätō). The color grey resists the concept of opposites and therefore hierarchy. This pertains most fully to the realm of mainstream biblical interpretation, which has advanced to the present by treating scriptural meaning as if it were black or white, right or wrong, true or false.

The color grey has no opposite. It is already a mixture of black and white. It is a spectrum devoid of absolutes. As such, grey can serve as a metaphor for thinking of theologies of scripture beyond orthodox/heretical, and interpretation beyond true/false.

To help us move boldly toward the fullness of life embodied in the way of Jesus, we will look at alternative ways of thinking about biblical meaning—making that participate in the semantic ambivalence, the multiple ways of meaning, arising out of scripture. The color grey is symbolic of biblical and theological work emerging from a philosophical/literary movement that began in the late 1960s called the "death of the author." This movement cleared the paths of biblical interpretation toward the "birth of the reader."

Such readings, because they are grounded in the concrete realities of human experience, make way for interpretations that are life-giving and love-bearing for those same communities and beyond. These contextual modes of interpretation in turn birthed new ways of understanding God found in liberation theologies of scripture. The greying of modes of biblical interpretation paints a picture, a way of understanding God's work in and through Holy Scripture that is neither black nor white.[3] This is a picture open to human flourishing and teeming with erotic potential.

Chapter Two

How to Get Away with Murder: The Death of the Author

To read the Bible today is not to decipher all by oneself a score
*   written by the very hand of the composer;*
it is to allow to come toward me that immense sonorous ocean
*   made of a thousand voices and*
a thousand instruments and to have the joy of becoming in it a
*   wavelet.*

— Jean-Louis Chrétien[1]

We cannot discern how God is so loving the world, how God is drawing abundant life out of death in and through scripture, if we refuse to listen. But the *how* of our listening is precisely the problem. How may we listen with the ears of love, opening our hearts and minds to the concrete realities of life, if mainstream modes of biblical interpretation are shouting at us all the while? How can any of us claim that scripture is life-giving when others find not freedom but bondage in the pages of scripture?

If we wish to embody the kind of love God displays toward creation, then we must find ways to listen to scripture without deciding in advance what scripture is allowed to mean. On a more fundamental level, we cannot approach God's Wor(l)d revealed in and through the Bible if we are unable to discern *how* the Bible means according to where and by whom it is read.

How about an illustration? We find a good one—juicy as your grandpappy's chaw—in Shonda Rhimes's latest hit television series, *How to Get Away with Murder.* The show features Professor Annalise Keating, a tough-as-nails criminal law professor at the fictional Middleton University in Philadelphia. Amidst Keating's racy personal and professional life, along with those of her law students, Rhimes offers us a way of thinking about making love with scripture vis-à-vis mainstream methods of biblical interpretation.

In the pilot episode, Keating teaches her first-year law students how *to get away with* murder. So, right out of the gate we witness a critical tension between winning one's case in the courtroom and fighting for justice (remember this; it will be on the test). Keating goes on to share her formula for winning a murder trial in three easy steps: 1) Discredit the witness; 2) Introduce a new suspect; and 3) Bury the evidence with so much information that the jury is filled with nothing but doubt. As an incentive for their hard work, Keating offers her students a chance at winning an "immunity idol" of sorts that will free them from an exam. This is her prize for the best defense. Ironically, this trophy is a bronze statue of Lady Justice.

In itself, the fact of human mortality is not that interesting. It's an unavoidable feature of life—"all men must die," *valar morghulis.* *lifts glass to George R. R. Martin; sips; chokes on poison; dies* Much more interesting are the conditions that shape our lives. How we live matters just as much, if not more, than what happens after we die. It doesn't mean that we shouldn't care about death. None of us wants to die. The mastery with which Rhimes entwines themes of life and death with legal prowess and actual justice presents a few questions for us to ponder: Do mainstream methods of biblical interpretation (aka "exegesis") promote life and justice, or might they inadvertently subvert love of God and neighbor? Are such methods akin to Keating's three easy steps, oriented more to winning one's case than seeking justice?

In spite of the inevitability of our deaths, much of our life's work is a marked attempt to stave off our demise. Whether through our children or our work, we desperately desire *not* to die, to live on somehow in spite of our inevitable passing. *gets sentimental; sings along to Jay Z's "Young Forever"; cries a little*

Something happened in France in the late-1960s that had a radical effect on literary theory and biblical studies. It started with an attack, wherein a group of philosophers and literary theorists—literarily, if not literally—got away with murder. This shift would come to be called "the death of the author." Hereafter, the scholarly attribution of biblical meaning could no longer center on the Bible's author, but on its reader, and eventually on the reading communities that sustain certain kinds of readings.

The author, as the governing factor in biblical interpretation, was murdered to set readers free. As student revolts were taking place in the Netherlands (1966) and France (1968), and social protests were changing the American cultural landscape (1955–1968), philosophers were hosting their own rebellion against the "tyranny of the text."[2] *dons Che Guevara T-shirt and red-starred beret; shouts "¡Viva la Revolución!"; gets shushed by beady-eyed librarian* It remains for us to determine whether the author's murder was just or unjust.

Even as young people were opening their minds to new sounds and psychedelic influences at Woodstock (1969), burning their undies at the Miss America Protest (1968), and demonstrating against American involvement in Vietnam (1968–1969), philosophers were laying the intellectual tracks for a new way of thinking about the relationship between authors, readers, and biblical texts. I invite you, ladies and gentlemen of the jury, to consider the evidence and determine for yourself if justice was on their side.

Let Me Tell You a Story: What Happens When We Read

Okay, I just handed you my copy of *Nineteen Eighty-Four* (I'll want it back). Well, go on. Read it. Once you open that first page and allow your mind to enter George Orwell's dystopia, once you expose yourself to the world of "newspeak" and "reality control," once you permit the cadences of "doublethink" into your head, several miraculous events take place.

For starters, as soon as you begin to read Orwell's haunting tale, his book ceases to exist. What I mean is that the *materiality* of the book—its paper and ink, its worn paper cover—vanishes before the story itself. It is impossible to live in the world of the text and the world of the reader simultaneously.

That's the miracle of a book. It waits there patiently for someone to come along and deliver it from its materiality.[3] Of course, the book is still there, in your hand; but it's no longer *merely* there. In a sense, the book is nowhere, for as long as you mentally tiptoe across Orwell's pages under the ubiquitous gaze of Big Brother, the book *as such* ceases to exist for you, the reader. All that matters to your consciousness is the "vivid and continuous dream" of the story itself, as novelist John Gardner once put it.

The "death of the author" is hugely important for contemporary biblical interpretation because it is first and foremost a liberation movement. You see, for centuries biblical scholars and theologians have restricted the range of biblical meaning according to the nebulous and dubious principle of "authorial intention." As you'll soon see, the "death of the author" liberates the Wor(l)d of God from its ideological constraints, thereby freeing us to see God's self-revelation in and through scripture in a whole new way.

No Longer "I": The Phenomenon of Reading

Reading exposes us to another person's consciousness and in the process places our own consciousness at risk. No prophylactic can safeguard our minds when we enter into the intellectual intercourse that is reading. Already in 1960, philosophers had argued that because everybody's consciousness is historically situated, readers are forever embroiled in cultural and historical situations. When we read, the "horizon" of our experiences fuses with those of the author whose work we are reading.[4]

Or think about it this way.

In reading, I'm aware of the consciousness of another person who is no different from the one I automatically assume in every human being I encounter, except in this case the consciousness of the person is *open* to me. The author's consciousness invites me in for tea; it allows me a long peek deep inside itself. When we read we enter the thoughts of another human being, and the more compelling those thoughts are for us, the more deeply we take on the author's thoughts as our own.

While we read, we also subject our thoughts to another. This is a trick played on the mind of the reader, for our consciousness behaves as though it were that of another. In other words, when we read, we loan our minds to an author, who is then permitted to populate our minds with her narrative imagination. It's a form of #Inception. In a sense, the ideas presented in a text belong to no one. As wind fills the sails of a mighty ship or propels a great windmill, the ideas of an author are there for me to use according to my good pleasure. They pass from the author to me as coins are passed from hand to hand.

It is only when I break the vivid and continuous dream that reading evokes—when I pause to reflect on *my* world of experience—that I am able to return to my consciousness. Upon scrutiny, I discover that even as my thoughts remain a part of *my* mental world, in reading I find myself thinking thoughts that manifestly belong to *another* mental world. The thoughts of the author are being thought in me just as though I did not exist. Thus, even as reading is life-giving, it also inaugurates a sort of death for the reader.

How 'bout an example?

In Stephanie Meyer's novel *The Host*, a teenage girl finds herself in a world that has been overtaken by an alien society. The aliens implant themselves within the minds of men, women, and children and proceed to use their bodies according to their own will.

Eventually, the story's protagonist, Melanie, is forced to play host to one of the aliens whom she nicknames "Wanda." The bulk of the story, and much of the tale's narrative drive, takes place in the tug-of-war that ensues over Melanie's consciousness between Melanie and Wanda. Later we learn that many human minds are inclined to submit to the alien invaders. But not Melanie. She is constantly fighting against the obliteration of her consciousness. The emotional climax of the story comes when Melanie and Wanda find a way to be at peace with each other.

Reading is a bit like this. Often, we completely submit to the mind of the author. Especially when we engage in "reading for pleasure," we read *in order to* escape the chaotic landscape of our minds, to silence the cacophony of our lives with the dulcet melodies of another. And especially when the writing is so good that it sweeps us in (bad writing often does just the opposite). In academic reading, on the other hand, we might be more like Melanie, raging against the mind of an author seeking to conform us to his or her perspective—um, yeah, like what I'm doing to you *right now*. *twists mustache*

Author? What Author?

Who then is really in control of the thoughts I experience when I read the work of another? Like fish in an aquarium, words, images, and ideas wriggle about in my mind. These mental entities, in order to exist, need the shelter that I provide; they are dependent on my consciousness. So, we can see that the text itself does not share the same relationship with me, the reader, as it does with the author who wrote the text. If a good story can cause me to forget myself, and even to forget that I exist as the one reading, how much more am I able to dismiss the author's presence?

The subject who presides over any work of literature can exist only *in* the work. The text is there, working its magic upon me. It does not exist to send me outside itself to its author, nor to other writings, but, on the contrary, to keep my attention riveted on the text itself. Pick up any book on fiction writing and it will tell you that the cardinal sin of writing is to draw unnecessary attention to yourself, the author. The writer exists to give life to the story, not to draw attention to himself—except when he doesn't, as in so-called postmodern fiction (e.g., Joyce's *Finnegan's Wake*, Pynchon's *Gravity's Rainbow*).

Another way of thinking about the author in regard to his work is that the author does not exist *outside* of it. The work is the sole means by which I have access to the author; but we have already seen how little the author as person matters to me *while* I am reading.

So, since the late-1960s, the author's significance has diminished. It will help if you think of those scenes in *Back to the Future* where Marty McFly starts to disappear from the photo in his puffy vest pocket when it seems that his parents will not hook-up at the Enchantment Under the Sea Dance. The author's presence was seen as fleeting by those on the cutting-edge of literary theory in the 1960s. What was left in the author's void was the writing itself and the reader's pleasure in reading the text.

What Would Jesus Do (with Scripture)?

You didn't buy this book to learn about literary theory. You want to learn how to make love with scripture, right? The "death of the author" campaign opens up biblical texts to myriad readings that would have been unthinkable with the author there, breathing his peanut butter breath over our shoulder. All that I have been showing philosophically can be seen within the Bible itself. Jesus himself didn't seem to place much stock in authorial intention (i.e., what Moses *meant*). He took great care, however, to see that scripture was put into practice *in the present*, that is, that our understanding of scripture is oriented toward life. Let's look at an example.

In Matthew's Gospel, just after Jesus shares his famous Beatitudes with his disciples, he tells them that he has not come to abolish or do away with the Hebrew Scriptures (the Law and the Prophets); instead he has come to fulfill them, that is, to carry them forward to completion (5:17). Jesus states explicitly his deep and abiding regard for Holy Scripture. And with the very next breath, Jesus tells his disciples, along with we who would listen, that the purpose of reading scripture is so that it may be accomplished *in* the reader. The Greek is stronger: until everything (in the scriptures) is brought to life.

Moving on, verse 20 reads, "For I tell you, unless your yearning for justice exceeds that of the scribes and Pharisees, you will never enter the kingdom of heaven." Jesus is telling us point-blank that the Hebrew religion is about *justice*. It's not just about what biblical texts meant in their historical context. Jesus' theology of scripture is about making the commandments of God and the call of the prophets materialize *today*. Jesus doesn't care that you were Bible Drill champion six years in a row. Jesus doesn't care if you can read Hebrew or Greek. Jesus makes love happen in and through his engagement with scripture. If you wish to be a Christ-follower, then that's what you need to do, too.

The rest of Matthew chapter 5 records Jesus riffing on the Hebrew Scriptures. "You have heard it said in ancient times, but I say to you . . ." Note that each of these themes from the Hebrew Scriptures that he retrieves and radicalizes has to do with how one treats others. Anger. Adultery. Divorce. Honesty. Retaliation. Love. These are the topics that Jesus reinterprets for his disciples.

Reading the Bible like Jesus means reading existentially, that is, reading in such a way that God's radical concern for the world takes shape in and through you, the reader.

Through Jesus' impromptu Bible lesson we also learn that we cannot separate love of God and love of neighbor, a point that Jesus will make explicit when he tells us that the greatest commandment is to love God *and* neighbor (Matt. 22:37). Here in chapter 5, Matthew's Jesus tells us that right relations with the other are requisite for proper worship of God (5:24). Thus, reading the Bible is just as much a world-oriented endeavor as it is God-oriented. Unless we discern in scripture how to make love manifest in our relations with human and nonhuman others, we are not reading the Bible like Jesus.

The Author Is Dead, Long Live the Reader

Thanks to "the death of the author" campaign, we can stop obsessing over the almighty and all-knowing capital-A Author, who gets to decide what his text means for all people and all times. We no longer must pay homage to a "figure" believed to exist outside of and antecedent to a text, and, as Jesus himself taught us, this includes the biblical text.[5]

In the wake of the author's death, we are freed to consider his or her writing without assigning a "secret," an ultimate meaning, to the text (and to the world as text). It saves us from deifying the author—as the islanders did Somni-451 in *Cloud Atlas*. The doctrine of the sovereignty of God that had been unwittingly transposed into the sovereignty of the capital-A Author can no longer abide (sorry, Dude!).

We need not fear this. Literary theory liberates us from projecting a god in our own image—the chief and most abominable, if not frequent, of sins.

To give writing its future requires us to overthrow the myth of a god-like Author who wields absolute control over a text's meaning:

"[T]he birth of the reader must be at the cost of the death of the Author."[6] The Author is a tyrant. He is neither divine nor is he able to stifle the proliferation of meanings that emerge from "his" texts. He is not the father and the text is not his child, and even if this were the case, such a child would be prodigal.

Here's the irony: The Author has always been evoked as a system of control. He is employed as "the principle of thrift" that restricts the possibility of meaning beyond approved, canonical interpretations. Asserting the Author's antecedence to his work allows him to be employed as a principle by which meanings are limited and even excluded, "in short, by which one impedes the free circulation, the free manipulation, the free composition, decomposition, and recomposition of fiction."[7] This is nothing less than the foundational operating assumption of mainstream biblical scholarship: "What Paul meant by this is X," "Jesus did not intend Y." This is unhelpful at best and blasphemous against the Holy Spirit at worst. Who are we to presume to speak for the God who works in and through scripture? To hell with such nonsense—literally!

Some fear that the author's demise creates an anything-goes, nihilistic, read-the-text-however-the-hell-you-want, ethic. Some worry that such an approach twists biblical meaning the way that Keating twists the law in *How To Get Away With Murder*. There's warrant for this fear; but that doesn't make the alternative option any better. How much worse is it to subvert justice just to maintain your group's interpretation—to win? Just because there is no one, "correct" meaning does not mean that there are no "incorrect" readings. To read the text out of irrational fear for its multiple ways of meaning and meaning potential in new contexts is just as wrong.

In the wake of the author's death we are freed to let the Wor(l)d of God revealed in and through scripture come alive in us—just like Jesus taught us. That is why the "death of the author" is so significant. By it we are free to show the world how scripture means by receiving it with gratitude and embodying it in love.

Chapter Three

99 Problems but the Text Ain't One: Cultural Interpretations of Scripture

Since we are different, we understand the text in a different
    way, or we do not
understand it at all. The lapse of time is not just a chasm to be
    overcome,
but is the occasion for productive understanding.
                                                    — AVERY DULLES[1]

Once the author is no longer sufficient to bludgeon biblical interpretations that diverge from those of mainstream biblical scholars, we are free to attend to scripture in many and varied ways.
Not only does the "death of the author" lead us toward a certain

interpretative freedom, it also allows us to listen to the call of those who have been objectified, marginalized, and mistreated by societal systems—systems in which Christianity in general and certain "Christian" interpretations of scripture are culpable.[2]

Jay Z (aka Shawn Carter), one of the most gifted rappers of all time, gives us a novel angle of vision on scripture, one that is sensitive to cultural particularities. His hypnotic flow and powerful lyrics have set a new standard for hip-hop art and expression. His most famous song is the 2004 hit, "99 Problems," arguably the most misunderstood song in his entire corpus.

Jay Z writes in his 2010 book, *Decoded*, that the song was never meant as a derogatory reference to women. In many ways, Jay Z explains, he was playing into the stereotype of his art, which was reinforced by critical reception of his work. The song is about racial profiling by the police and the gritty reality of hustling to make it on the streets and in the entertainment industry.

The song is based off of a real-life situation in which Jay Z found himself during the mid-nineties. He was pulled over for "driving while black." He refused to get out of the car and the police officer called in the K-9 unit, which would give the police probable cause to search Jay's vehicle for drugs, or so he reasons.

The song is ironic on multiple levels. Jay Z was pulled over for no other reason than the color of his skin ("You was doin' fifty-five in a fifty-four"). At the same time, he was guilty; he *did* have a stash of cocaine hidden in the sunroof of his Nissan Maxima. As he states in *Decoded*, "It is a story about the anxiety of hustling, the way little moments can suddenly turn into life-or-death situations. It's about being stopped by cops with a trunk full of coke, but also about the larger presumption of guilt from the cradle that leads you to have the crack in your trunk in the first place."[3]

"99 Problems" is a song about the commodification of black bodies, that is, about objectifying black bodies as *objects* of suspicion that require surveillance and discipline, and as com-modities in the billion-dollar-a-year hip-hop industry. It's about the harsh realities of what systems of inequity force young men to do to make a living, and the lack of justice perpetrated by law enforcement officers on men and women of color—as the recent incidents in Ferguson, Long Island, and Baltimore have made unquestionably clear.

Many people suffer from marginalization and oppression by the reigning power structures that claim to be blind to color, sexu-ality, and ethnicity and are anything but. There's a reason that "99 Problems" is listed as the #2 greatest song of the 2000s by *Rolling Stone* magazine: it poignantly captures something of our Western ethos and refuses to bend over and take it.

Marginalized persons in general and African Americans in particular face many problems in the U.S.—*but the text ain't one.* In spite of racist and oppressive interpretations that subordinate and marginalize black bodies, the Bible has long been a source of empowerment and resistance. From African American spiritu-als that took on the language of biblical texts, mixing their own interpretations out of their horrendous experiences of suffering and oppression, to the Jazz and Blues appropriations of the same, African Americans have long drawn upon the Bible as a powerful source of hopefulness.[4]

At the same time, the meaning of biblical texts ain't *one*. Like Katy Perry's hair color, biblical texts are always under negotiation, and history itself bears witness to the fact that biblical meaning is constantly reframed by contextual circumstances. Textual mean-ing arises out of the dynamic interplay between scripture and the lived experiences of participants in various communities. People find in the Bible different ways of meaning, meanings open to human flourishing and communities working to subvert societal norms and injustices. That is why we must listen to such voices; it is a necessary first step toward loving one's neighbor as oneself.

Is There a Text in This Church?
Cultural Interpretation

Like the grooming habits of Chewbacca, biblical interpretation is marked by both its necessity and messiness. *Aaaaaaaaaaaarrrgh!* That's Wookie for "Don't hate the playa; hate the game." Biblical meaning doesn't just happen. It arises out of a community's lived experience with the God revealed in and through scripture.

In terms of discerning a text's meaning, we have already seen that the reader is born out of the author's demise. Once the author is no longer regarded as the arbiter of the so-called "proper" understanding of his work, readers are free to interpret texts out of their lived realities. Accompanying the reader's mode of interpretation (i.e., the ways of meaning-making she distills from biblical texts) is the reading community. It takes a village to raise an interpretation.[5] Said differently, no interpretation of scripture takes shape apart from a community of interpretation—the people, circumstances, and life-experiences that shape her understanding. As the reader's contextual circumstances change, so must her interpretation.

But here's the thing. We are not limited to the meanings arising out of our own church communities and cultural contexts. New Testament scholar Brian Blount is right to note that "the fullest possible meaning can be achieved only by drawing from the variety of interpretations, not understanding them as alternatives, but as providing a complementary range of meaning."[6] In other words, we who would seek to love our neighbor as ourselves in and through scripture must open ourselves to readings that emerge from different cultural spaces. We must expand our interpretive worldview, so to speak.

But this raises a problem. If there is no one "correct" meaning, does that mean that *all* meanings are equally valid? Are we to leave it to the loudest voices to set the interpretive standards in the theological marketplace? Are the biblical interpretations of Rev. Dr. Martin Luther King Jr. on equal ground with the folks at

Westboro Baptist Church? Is Westboro's "God Hates Fags" campaign on par with King's "Beloved Community"?

By no means! Holy Scripture is not an all-you-can-eat salad bar, where you are free to eat whatever the hell you feel like eating. We are theologically and morally responsible for our interpretations. Because, love. Love and the flourishing of life set the standard. Any biblical interpretation worthy of the name must make "a pact of blood with the world."[7] This is our standard, the litmus test if you will for adjudicating among various interpretations: Does this interpretation foster greater love of God and neighbor in the concrete, political circumstance of life? If your answer to this question is "no," then let it go like the *Frozen* soundtrack. And all the parents say, "Amen!"

I Have the Power: Discerning Abundant Life

It's about as tenuous as a *Transformers* plot arc to stress the importance of concrete, culturally situated modes of biblical interpretation in an abstract, philosophical sense. Only by attending closely to the ways scripture means from community to community, from person to person, can we begin to grasp the theological significance of contextual interpretations.

Hospitality over Whoring: A Queer Womanist Reading of Numbers 25

Numbers 25:1-8 is an odd passage of scripture wedged in between Balaam's prophecies and a scene of Technicolor gore on par with the *300*—though with fewer six-packed dudes in banana hammocks.[8] It describes what happens when the Israelites begin to have "unsanctioned-intimate-relationships" with the women of Moab as they are wandering about in the wilderness in search of the "Promised Land." Many mainstream biblical commentators are quick to register God's anger resulting from the people's worship of Baal of Peor, and then breeze on to the bloodlust of Phinehas, son of Aaron the priest.[9] Is that it? Case closed? Does God command racism along with theological fidelity?

Some think not.

The challenges of negotiating cultural identity are stated clearly and insightfully by Hebrew Bible scholar Wil Gafney.[10] Out of her African American cultural context, Gafney offers what she labels a "womanist midrash" on Num. 25:1-8—btw, midrash is not *that* kind of rash; it's a form of biblical commentary that is attached to the biblical text. No penicillin required. Through Gaffney's contextually situated interpretive engagement, we gain deeper insight into how gender, race, and sexuality shape biblical interpretation.

Numbers 25 opens with the hard-working, God-fearing Israelites chillaxing in a region called Shittim (no comment, seriously not gonna touch that one, too easy). While encamped there, the Israelites begin to have "unsanctioned-intimate-relationships" with the women of Moab and to worship these foreign gods. Gafney begins by noting how strange this scenario is.

Israelite men frequently took non-Israelite women as wives. Moses did. At times God even sanctioned the abduction of women and girls of non-Israelite peoples as breeding stock.[11] Gafney suggests that what is particularly odd about this passage is that the "people" of Israel are having "unsanctioned-intimate-relationships" with the women of Moab. Gafney makes a compelling grammatical and narrative case for her interpretation, noting that the Hebrew term translated as "people" is used broadly in the book of Numbers. Thus, it appears that men *and* women were entwined in these "unsanctioned-intimate-relationships," which seems to present one of the only cases of women's same-gender sexual activity in the Hebrew Bible.

Moving on, Gafney observes that one of the interpretative keys to this text is the identity of the Moabite god. The Hebrew word that is employed in verse 2 can be rendered as a singular or plural noun: *god* or *gods*. The traditional translations opt for the plural noun, emphasizing the difference between the singular Israelite God (which, btw, also has a plural ending in Hebrew). This translation conceals an interpretive decision.

Against the grain of mainstream interpretations, Gafney sees the inaugurated community of Moabite women and Israelite women and men representative of a type of womanist community, that is, one committed to survival and wholeness.[12] She notes that the Moabite women mentioned in Numbers 25 are incontestably *other*, both in terms of their African descent and in terms of their cultural differences. From her womanist frame of meaning-making, Gafney argues that the Moabite women offered sacred hospitality, a space of belonging, a kind of "women's culture" that is radically inclusive. For this they ought to be celebrated, not impaled (vv. 4, 7-8).

She concludes that what makes Numbers 25 a "queer" text is not the possibility of same-gender sexual contact between women, but the choice of an untold number of the Israelite people to forsake their pilgrimage and their prophets for a different promise, namely, one of radical inclusion. It's not really about who's banging whom; it's about who *belongs* to whom. It's less about whoring than hospitality—a biblical mandate, I believe. Here Gafney offers us a clear depiction of a womanist interpretation, one that finds room for multiple voices and makes room for the other. Her reading prompts a serious theological question: What truly ought we regard as "unsanctioned": hospitality or xenophobia? Gafney's reading passes the test of love because it reads the text with an orientation to the other beyond religious and cultural taboos and anxieties.

God's Supreme Justice: Reading the Parable of the Vineyard Laborers

From a very different contextual space, Latino church historian and theologian Justo González offers a striking interpretation of Jesus' parable of the laborers in the vineyard (Matt. 20:1-16) from an explicitly liberationist theology of scripture. He opens his reflections by noting that interpretations of this parable arising out of a middle-class perspective share little in common with either of the two social classes to which Jesus' parable refers: the rich landowner and the poor day-laborer, servant, or peasant.

When most middle-class Christians read this parable—wherein the owner of the vineyard pays all workers the same wage regardless of the time spent in the fields—they see this as an egregious display of unfairness. "It is just not right," González writes, "that people who worked more should be paid the same as people who worked less."[13] From a middle-class perspective, all that is seen is the glaring injustice, and concomitant sermons in such contexts, González argues, state that God's grace is above justice.

We should pause here and observe that the middle-class interpretation is grounded in a certain economic situation that privileges compensation in proportion to work performed, which masks a sociopolitical ideology presupposing a scenario in which jobs are readily available for any who wish to work. Thus, the actions of the landowner are not read as compensational, but as displays of welfare, or worse, socialism. *Dun-dun-duuun!*

González sees things differently.

He notes that when this parable is read in impoverished Latin@ (i.e., Latino/Latina) churches, it is received with joy. You see, such people can readily identify with the laborers. They understand the plight of those who must rise early in the morning to stand outside Home Depot, waiting in the hope that someone will come along in an F-150 pickup truck and hire them for the day. If they are lucky, they will find a whole day's work. Other days, they may spend hours waiting without being hired, or they may only be hired for a few hours.

The surprising twist in Jesus' parable comes not as a shock of horror, but of jubilation.[14] The landowner pays those who only worked a couple of hours a full day's wage! González explains that from an economically marginalized position people are able to see that those who have been "standing here idle all day" (Matt. 20:6) had done so not on account of their laziness or lack of desire to work; rather, they exhibited *more* hope and stamina to remain than those who were hired first thing in the morning.

González concludes by writing that just because no one hired them doesn't mean that they don't have to eat, or that their needs are less. Everyone needs a full day's wage to survive. Therefore, when the landowner pays everyone a full day's wage, it's not a show of grace that goes against justice. This radical display of grace understands justice at the deepest level: "The landowner pays them what they justly need and what they justly deserve, not what society, with its twisted understanding of justice, would pay them."[15]

González's interpretation participates in the liberationist orientation of many Latin@ readers. His angle of vision on this text challenges readings from affluent communities that know nothing of the existential pains of subsistence in today's globalized economies. Because it is oriented to the abundant life necessary for loving one's neighbor as oneself, it is a reading that passes the most strident of tests, the test of love.

Unity amidst Difference: Reconfiguring Difference in Galatians

Let's look at a final concrete example of a culturally situated reading in action. This example is articulated by New Testament scholar Brad Braxton in his book, *No Longer Slaves: Galatians and African American Experience.*[16]

Braxton draws explicitly upon and makes overt reference to his experiences as an African American man, and his cultural location finds deep meaning in one, well-known passage of scripture, Galatians 3:28: "There is no longer Jew or Greek, there is no longer slave or free, there is no longer male and female; for all of you are one in Christ Jesus" (NRSV).

Braxton begins by challenging the assumption of some that Paul's declaration in verse 28 should be read as an eschatological ideal—a laudable goal that will only be fully accomplished upon the return of Christ. Braxton vigorously questions this assumption on rhetorical and grammatical grounds established throughout Paul's letter to the church at Galatia.

Next, Braxton dismisses the misconception that Christian unity implies or entails the absence or abolishment of social distinctions. He explains that proponents of this view believe that unity in the church is achieved through eradicating social distinctions and replacing them with an amalgamated "colorblind" Christian identity.

Braxton confronts this view on two fronts. First, he contends that it is impossible to ignore socially constructed difference. Second, he rightly notes that such a reading contradicts many other passages in the letters of Paul, passages that seem to embrace ethnic difference. Such a reading participates in the lived experience of African Americans who continue to experience societal marginalization, objectification, and outright abuse in spite of supposed legal protection.

Having set the stage, Braxton then explains that when Paul says "there is neither Jew nor Greek, there is neither slave nor free, there is neither male and female," he is not asserting "the obliteration of difference, but rather the obliteration of dominance."[17] Braxton continues, arguing that our unity in Christ does not consist in an amalgamated or undifferentiated identity. Instead, we are rightly "one in Christ" because each Christian individual and each Christian community has a relationship in faith with Christ, and these faith(ful) relationships with Christ are meant to ensure that we relate to each other, in the midst of our many differences, "with mutuality and equality."

Braxton observes that Christ has freed the African American to affirm his or her blackness. Historically, he notes, blackness has been despised. Arguments for a specious and artificial unity promoted in certain circles that claim that blackness may be ignored are just as insidious. He concludes, "All Americans (and certainly all Christians) should strive for unity, but genuine unity will emerge from a dialogue among culturally distinct groups. Like textual meaning, racial unity is not discovered; it is created or bursts into existence."[18]

One need not strain to consider how the marginalization of men and women of color serves the ascendancy of Caucasians. Braxton's reading teaches us that interpretations that advocate ignoring race under the banner of Christian unity reinforce the economic, educational, and political disparities between those in positions of power and those with little or no power. By contrast, his cultural interpretation serves the real-world conditions of African Americans by urging mutuality and equality as the true meaning and manifestation of unity in Christ. Thus, Braxton's reading passes the test of love, opening us to be lovingly *for* the other.

Found in Translation: The Values and Risks of Contextual Interpretation

We learn nothing from these examples of contextual interpretations if not this: The text ain't the problem. We are. Scripture remains constant, for the most part. The dynamism of scripture to which we point when we say "the Word of God for the people of God" loses all meaning when we don't regard the Bible as at least as dynamic as our lived experiences in the world. It is imperative for we who would make love with scripture to read interpretations of scripture from those who do not share our ethnic, gender, racial, economic, etc. conditions so that we can see *what else* the scripture might have to say beyond our own contexts.

But we take on certain risks when we expose ourselves to alternative readings. Nearly as pernicious as disregarding biblical interpretations that don't share your cultural assumptions is the sin of valorizing every reading but your own. Other readings from different spaces can call our ideological and theological assumptions into question. This is a good thing. It opens us up to receive the neighbor in love. At the same time, we can commit the same error of contextually dislocated interpretations of scripture when we put the interpretations of other communities up on a pedestal. We must allow ourselves to be truly challenged by alternative interpretations of the Bible, not so that we can assimilate or co-opt these readings into our own practices of interpretation, but to experience the call of the neighbor directed at us in and through scripture.

Okay, you ask, how do we do this? I answer: You gotta put on your dancing shoes. First, we ought to begin from a place of radical openness to readings that emerge out of cultural and ideological contexts different from our own. Second, we must submit all interpretations—our own first and foremost—to rational, theological, and ethical critique.[19] I like to call these the retreat and the advance. Together they make up the dance of biblical interpretation. *breaks into Harlem shake; daughter rolls her eyes*

The first movement of contextual interpretations is the retreat, particularly for those whose interpretative practices have been favored by mainstream methods of biblical interpretation. By this you create a space in yourself to encounter the ideas of another in their otherness, that is, without trying to wrangle them into line with your categories and terminology. This movement leads you to resist the temptation to reduce otherness to sameness, to coopt the work of the other.

This gesture of retreat is one of both hospitality and empathy, wherein I play host to the other and seek to discern what is true, beautiful, and life-giving in her reading. It involves a fervent listening, not just a listening to what is said, but to the pains and hopes, fears, and desires that reside *behind* what is said.

Such a retreat is made possible only when I bracket my ideological and cultural assumptions, including my thoughts about *what* a particular passage of scripture might mean. The issue here is not *what* the text means but *how* the text means for the other.

The second movement is that of the advance, which might be the first movement for those whose reading practices have been marginalized by mainstream methods of biblical interpretation. This gesture is directed *toward* the other. It demands a critical eye that is able to look beyond a generous reception of another's interpretation. It's a mode of engagement by which you ask the hard questions of a text and inquire into those ideological assumptions that lurk behind every interpretation—BTW, ideology is shorthand for the cultural, psychological, aesthetic, linguistic, political, and even theological commitments that the reader brings to bear on biblical interpretation. Ideology is neither inherently good nor inherently bad. It just is—like Zach Galifianakis's beard.

The movement of advance does not negate the first movement of retreat, but draws it into critical tension. The advance not only attends to the underlying assumptions of an interpretation but also to the fruit such interpretations produce. As theologian Tony Jones puts it, "Bad theology begets ugly Christianity. Good theology begets beautiful Christianity." Jones calls this the "smell test," and it's one that can serve us well as we challenge the theological and ethical implications of acts of interpretation, which for me is the test of love.[20]

The dance of cultural interpretations is not without its risks. What if we are actually converted by another's interpretation? This is indeed a risk we take, but it only feels risky within a cultural context that is suspicious of otherness. This fear is misguided.

Taking the time to understand how different people read the Bible in different ways does not mean that you have to accept everything they say as 100 percent certified, grade-A gospel. At the same time, to reiterate, exposure to another's interpretation does not mean that I should adopt another's interpretation as my own. It is disingenuous for me, given my cultural rootedness, to take on the interpretation of another as my own without careful acknowledgment of the differences that remain in spite of whatever theological confluence may emerge. If I do this, I am "reaping what I did not sow," as the master does in Jesus' parable of the talents in Matthew 25.

What we need are reading practices and theologies of scripture that appreciate difference without co-opting it, taming it, or making it suitable to my purposes. We require a way of thinking about God's Wor(l)d rooted in the particular—and the particular always arises out of a particular context; that's precisely what makes it particular.

Chapter Four

Sméagol Knows the Way: Liberation Theologies of Scripture

Anyone who permits another to determine the quality of his
* inner life*
gives into the hands of the other the keys to his destiny.
— HOWARD THURMAN[1]

Remember the chicken-egg analogy I used in the Introduction? It's how biblical interpretations relate to theologies of scripture. Well, if our readings of scripture are shaped by our contextual circumstances, then those same circumstances will inform how we understand God's work in and through our engagement with scripture.

Does this mean that our concrete experiences determine who God is for us? Yeppers! Of course the *for us* is crucial because just as no one holds the one, true meaning of a biblical text, nobody has unfettered access to God. Anyone who claims they can let you in on the secret of God's existence is probably trying to sell you something.

The secret is there is no Secret.[2] But don't tell anyone I told you this. It's a secret.

For all intents and purposes, there is no capital-S Secret to unlocking the mystery presented to us in the name "God." In the same way that there is no capital-A Author who can secure a text's capital-M Meaning, we have no conceptualization of God that is not an interpretation. Faith in God is interpretation all the way down. You can't see God, and so you walk by faith.

But also like biblical interpretations, not all notions of God are equally beneficial or just. The question we must ask ourselves is how a certain listening to the concrete realities of life might provide understandings of God that are more life-giving and love-bearing. That's what love is all about, right? Loving is first and foremost listening. It follows that if we really want to love our neighbors as ourselves, then we will listen, really listen, to the cries of injustice and oppression of all people, even if it challenges our perception of God. And then we will respond to those cries in love.

Moving from the "death of the author" through contextual modes of interpretation, we are in a better position to understand *how* God means in and through scripture. To get to this will require that we clear a space to listen to how people from different gender, sexual, ethnic, racial, etc. circumstances understand God and how such a mode of vision might open us up to making love with God in and through scripture.

To move us in this direction, how 'bout an illustration? One of the most complex characters in J. R. R. Tolkien's *Lord of the Rings* saga is an emotionally volatile and psychically haunted character named Sméagol. In Tolkien's narrative universe, Sméagol (who is also called Gollum) is the object of universal scorn and mistreatment. Everywhere in Middle Earth he finds himself on the underside of political and social systems, and to add injury to insult, he is perpetually tormented by the psychic damage resulting from his long possession of the One Ring—a symbol of the will to power forged to facilitate the Dark Lord Sauron's ascendancy.

By my interpretation, the One Ring incarnates the drive to dominate others, to bend them to one's will, to use others as means to one's ends. In the hands of Sméagol, a simple and peaceful Hobbit reared along the Anduin River in the Gladden Fields, the innate power of the One Ring was like a drug. It poisoned his mind because it twisted a drive for external domination inward, causing him to feast on his own sense of self-worth. #whydoeshecry?

Sméagol features prominently in one of the central plot arcs of *Lord of the Rings*, which follows the quest of Frodo and Sam to destroy the One Ring and thereby vanquish Sauron, the Ring's creator. To destroy the One Ring, the Hobbits must make the perilous and arduous journey to Mordor, a desolate land where the very incarnation of evil dwells.

At a pivotal scene in *Lord of the Rings*, Sméagol has fulfilled his charge to lead Frodo and Sam to the Black Gate—the Morannon—the most fortified and direct entrance into the land of Mordor. When Frodo and Sam proceed to storm the keep, Sméagol stops them. He tells them of another path into Mordor: "Another way, darker, more difficult to find, more secret. But Sméagol knows it. Let Sméagol show you."

Here's the point for us to consider from *Lord of the Rings* (beyond teaching us the value of second breakfast, of course): Sméagol knew the way into Mordor because he himself had found a way to "escape" it. Having been tortured both physically and psychically by the agents of Sauron, Sméagol had experienced the sorrow and hopelessness of subjugation. He found a way out, but he is forever marked by the spiritual, psychological, and physical scars of his captivity; they define him.

In a similar sense, although we must not press this analogy too far, Sméagol illustrates the plight of liberation theologians, particularly those who have endured marginalization and oppression on account of their differences (e.g., racial, economic, sexual) from those in power.

Liberation theologies arise out of communities that have faced similar experiences of humiliation and degradation. Out of such suffering comes a certain knowledge, a certain way of seeing the world, including the world of the biblical text. As Costa Rican theologian Elsa Tamez puts it, the poor and oppressed are in a privileged place to interpret scripture because they are able to see clearly God's "preferential option" for those on the margins.[3] They also help the rest of us to see God's concern beyond those concerns that get Donald Trump all flushed and frothy.

It is in this sense that oppressed and marginalized persons know the way to interpret scripture oriented to love of neighbor. They know those "darker" and "more secret" paths that bypass the imposing and impregnable "front gate" of biblical meaning offered by mainstream modes of interpretation. And let we who are *Lord of the Rings* fans never forget that it was Sméagol—not the mighty Aragorn, not the sagacious Gandalf, not the resourceful Frodo— who actually destroyed the One Ring—oops, spoiler alert!

For Fullness of Life: Liberation Theologies and the Bible

Christian social ethicist Miguel De La Torre offers a definition of liberation theology that is as straightforward as you'll find. He explains that liberation theology is a "faith that raises consciousness" and that strives against the sociopolitical, economic, and theological modes of oppression inflicted upon the powerless.[4] What unifies liberation theologies in spite of their contextual differences is that they unabashedly situate God on the side of the oppressed and marginalized, seeking abundant life for all people.

Christian liberation theologies are rooted in the way of God arising out of God's boundary-breaking, life-giving Word revealed in scripture. Liberation theologians are nearly unanimous on this point. As theologian James Cone writes, "It is indeed the biblical witness that says that God is a God of liberation, who speaks to the oppressed and abused, and assures them that divine righteousness will vindicate their suffering."[5] Preach, Dr. Cone! *Woot! Woot!*

Oh, and they didn't just make this stuff up.

Jesus was a liberation theologian. He said, "I have come that they might have life and have it more abundantly" (John 10:10). It is the only understanding of God's way of being with the created order that fosters love of neighbor. Period. *drops microphone. exits stage* We can't claim to love our neighbor and then situate our understanding of God in some pie-in-the-sky-by-and-by ideal, an otherworldly sentiment beyond the real suffering of men, women, and children. To ignore God's promise of abundant life is to misunderstand Jesus' entire life and ministry, the Law, and the Prophets.

Theologies of liberation seek to understand the faith from within the concrete historical circumstances of human beings. Theology comes *after* involvement. It's a "second act." The themes of liberation theologies are often the same as more traditional theologies (e.g., creation, salvation, eschatology), but their focus and manner of approaching these concepts is different.[6] It is this different relationship with historical involvement that sets liberation theologies apart from so-called "theology" proper. Walking with God in the world discloses a way of seeing God in scripture. Oh, snap! *commences finger-whipping* Needle that onto your granny's throw-pillow—or on her arm, if she's that kind of granny!

All theologies of scripture emerge out of life. Theology is never neutral or objective. The difference between liberationist theologies of scripture and so-called "objective" or "universal" theologies of scripture is the deliberate inclusion of one's cultural and political context upon one's engagement with scripture. Liberation theologies offer the most faithful approach to love of God and neighbor in and through scripture; hence, they merit our attention.

Lady Lumps: Feminist Theologies of Scripture

Throughout recorded history women have been, and continue to be, oppressed by men, because, let's be honest, men can be dicks. Tragically, women have taken their lumps, so to speak, because men are capable of monstrous acts. Seriously. Google it.

As horrendous as the pervasiveness of domestic violence and rape are, the psychic damage women have suffered through their societal marginalization has also been, and continues to be, traumatic. For much of human history women have had no recourse but to accept their status as the "second sex."[7] Feminist theologies of scripture paint a different picture.

Alongside their Latino and African American brothers, many white feminist theologians draw from the deep reservoir of scripture to articulate their theological claims. Accordingly, feminist theologies of scripture challenge patriarchy, male-centeredness, and misogyny in the Bible, offering modes of interpretation oriented toward women's liberation.

Feminist theologies that hold scripture as a resource for women's empowerment regard the Bible as the seedbed of abundant life. When read through the path of women's historical experience, the Bible can be a means of liberation. This requires a certain mode of reading biblical texts, for even though egalitarian impulses are discernible in the Bible, the texts as such were written mostly by dudes for dudes. Feminist liberation interpretations arise out of a feeling of ambivalence toward the biblical witness, and oftentimes toward the God witnessed by scripture. As Elisabeth Schüssler Fiorenza, arguably the most prolific and forceful feminist biblical scholar, puts it, "the source of our power is also the source of our oppression."[8]

Scripture itself fosters ambivalence. For even though feminine imagery is employed for understanding God, the dominant mode of expressing God in scripture is masculine—the Divine *He*. When biblical words and metaphors are equated with God's self-revelation, the human modes of conveying God's self-revelation can also be viewed as inspired. This theological Dutch oven has noxious effects for all people.[9] Feminist theologies of scripture teach us to separate masculine expressions of God from God's self-revelation—an essential distinction to be sure. So, for instance, feminist theologians would hold Jesus' frequent references to God as Father in John's Gospel lightly, seeing in it more of a relational than gendered quality.

Feminist theologies of scripture offer us a theological vision for interpreting scripture that resists male domination and female subjugation. They teach us to read between the lines of texts, searching for invisible, unnamed women, listening for their muted voices. As such, feminist theologies find in scripture a way toward women's flourishing.

La Raza: Latin American Theologies of Scripture

God dwells among the poor and marginalized. That's where Jesus spent almost all of his time, and that is where we who hope to follow God in the way of Jesus Christ must go.[10] Accordingly, the economically and racially marginalized of Latin America have an utterly different vision of God than those of us reared in conditions of power and privilege—our only threat being those sentient Krispy Kreme doughnuts bent on global domination.

At the point of power and privilege is where we find the essential thrust of Latin American liberation theologies of scripture. They show us a God who displays a "preferential option for the poor and oppressed." They teach us that the way of God in Jesus calls for a living commitment to *do* theology, to strive toward justice, to fight for the fullness of life for all God's children.

Latin American liberation theologies move from reflection on lived experience toward the biblical text. When you start with your eyes wide open to the suffering and silencing of people, you are able to read scripture with "new eyes." This fresh vision then allows you to imagine alternative modes of being beyond the nightmare of oppression and marginalization. This way of seeing allows Latin American liberation theologians to assert themselves right where theory (faith) and practice (love) intersect.[11] Scripture is their Indiana Jones whip. *Pshhhh.*

Scripture holds a pride of place for Latin American liberation theologies.[12] Most regard the Bible as the primary means by which modern persons may understand God and ourselves. Scripture shows us who God is toward us—that God is radically *for* us in Jesus Christ, and particularly for those on the margins of society. It is in scripture that we discover our identity (as God's beloved), our purpose (to foster a new humanity under the auspices of God's peaceful kingdom), and the central message of the gospel (liberation for all people). Scripture is the *source* of theological and political engagement.

Latin American liberation theologies of scripture teach us that the ultimate basis of God's preference for the poor is found in God's goodness, not in social analysis or in human agency. It is the Wor(l)d of God read with an awareness of the plight of the poor and oppressed that structures an interpretive orientation toward liberation. The liberation theologian goes to the scriptures bearing the weight of the concerns, sorrows, and hopes of the poor, seeking light and inspiration from God's Wor(l)d. Such theologies are equal parts flick to the ear of a-political biblical interpretations and a grenade under the pew of dispassionate social engagement.

La Lucha: Mujerista Theologies of Scripture

Mujerista theologies of scripture attend to the living and reading strategies employed by American women of Latin American descent as well as Latinas/Hispanas worldwide. As one of the most marginalized and impoverished people groups in the world, Latinas have a particular angle of vision on Jesus' life and ministry that shapes their sociopolitical outlook as well as their ways of interpreting scripture—indeed, the two are inseparable.

Mujerista (*mujer* means "woman" in Spanish) theologies are not only concerned with the betterment of the lives of Latinas. Ada María Isasi-Díaz, the progenitor of *mujerista* theology, explains it like this: "*Mujerista* theology seeks to contribute to the elaboration of 'reality-based universals' open to differences and diversity, seeking to include instead of excluding, reconciling instead of establishing hegemonic understandings that promote the privileges of the few at the expense of the many."[13] To be sure, *Mujerista* theologies are equal parts Care Bear and Wonder Woman, showing compassion even as they fight for truth and justice. *slips into Care Bear furry costume and plays with collection of vintage Wonder Woman action figures* What? Don't judge me.

Mujerista theologies of scripture are more than a mash-up of feminist and Latin American theologies. To be sure, *Mujerista* theologies of scripture arose in the 1980s out of a dissatisfaction with feminist theology's failure to deal sufficiently with racial and class differences and Latin American theology's failure to confront its inherent misogyny. But race and sex add up to more than the sum of their parts. This calls for a more nuanced understanding of God and neighbor.[14]

Unsurprisingly, the Bible is rarely the focal point of *mujerista* theologies of scripture. Rather, *mujerista* theologians acknowledge that they "struggle to discern how to appropriate and use the Bible," contending that scripture doesn't get to Pass Go or collect $200. It's owed the same liberationist critique as all of life's structures.[15] Many *mujerista* interpreters are able to see that the Word of God (*la palabra de Dios*) is not necessarily what is written in the Bible. For them, the Word of God refers to the God who is "with us in our daily struggles."[16]

This does not mean, however, that the Bible is not an important conversation partner for Latinas. Some Latina biblical scholars have expressed a relationship to the Bible using the language of homelessness or exile, a "reading from no place," where one's ethnic, racial, and gender position in her community is in a constant state of flux and negotiation. Living "in the hyphen," between eth-nic identities in the U.S. context, structures a relationship with the biblical text where communal and theological boundaries are continually being redrawn.[17]

Along with matters of race and gender, *mujerista* theologies of scripture attend to economic disparities that shape biblical inter-pretation. Theirs is an interpretation that refuses to remain docile and instead, rejects systems of thought and images that fail to fur-ther the liberation of *mujeristas*.[18] The powerfulness of such read-ings makes Lara Croft look like Taylor Swift.

Black Power: African American Theologies of Scripture

African American liberation theologies (aka "black theologies") aim to restore to African Americans a "God-revealed conscious-ness," namely, a theologically oriented self-understanding of the inherent goodness and worth of black bodies and minds amidst white oppression.[19] This is precisely what African American the-ologies of scripture have done and continue to do.

Theologian Tupac Shakur says, "All I see is racist faces. Mis-placed hate makes disgrace to races." Umm. *checks notes* Damn it, who wrote these? Theologian James Cone writes, "This is black liberation, the emancipation of black minds and black souls from white definitions of black humanity."[20] Yeah, that's what I meant. Cone urges African Americans to assume the dominant role in determining black-white relationships in U.S. society, to adopt an *attitude*—an existential and collective affirmation of the essential worth of men and women of color.[21]

African American liberation theologies offer an alternative intellectual framework, one that refuses to capitulate to Western modes of thought and discourse. Cone labels this "Black Power." It's a theological middle finger to Western rationality. He argues that such systems of thought and practice further bolster a certain (white) way of being in the world while simultaneously denigrating black rage at the absurdity of subjugated existence. For Cone, all "God-talk" ought to be "black-talk," and the task of black theologies ought to be that of analyzing the lived experiences and psychic pressures of African Americans in light of God's revelation in Jesus Christ.[22]

Flowing from African American liberation theologies is an Afrocentric orientation toward biblical interpretation, one in which such lived experience is "not only recognized but embraced and celebrated."[23] This charge has been led by Prof. Vincent Wimbush, whose writings on Afrocentric modes of interpretation attend not only to the texts themselves, but to what he labels "scripturalization." This refers to "the ideology and power dynamics and social and cultural practices built around texts," in short, the "magic" the Bible performs upon society.[24]

African American liberation theologies of scripture are oriented toward the existential, spiritual, and material deliverance of men and women of color. It is a mode of reading the Bible that is at once aware of the history of slavery and oppression of African Americans, troubled by the continued economic disparities facing persons of color, and oriented toward liberation.

Àṣẹ!: *Womanist Theologies of Scripture*

The designation "womanist" was developed by Alice Walker to differentiate the lived realities of African American women from those of white feminists, on the one hand, and African American men, on the other.[25] Womanist scholars present a wide array of perspectives on the appropriate theological approach to oppressive systems of injustice. What unifies womanist theologies of scripture is that all read the Bible in light of the plight of African American women amidst corporate, political, and ecclesial systems of oppression.[26]

Acquiescing to systems of power that reinforce domination according to race, sex, and class can cause one to lose her "critical consciousness."[27] In her landmark text, *Talking Back*, bell hooks claims a ground for the voices of black women. It is a mode of bold, defiant speech. Such discourse, such a "gesture of defiance," brings healing even as it makes "new life and new growth possible."[28] Accordingly, womanist theologies of scripture offer a theological and interpretative approach for moving from silence into speech in and through scripture.

In response to the lived realities of African American women, womanist theologies of scripture fight against structures of self-understanding that do not foster the inherent goodness of African American women.[29] Drawing deeply from scripture, womanist theologies proclaim the inherent goodness and worth of all people. This mode of scriptural engagement is life-affirming for African American women, leading them to God's claim upon their lives in resistance to societal structures that would lay claim to their identity.

Hebrew Bible scholar Renita Weems offers a helpful example of what a womanist theology of scripture looks like. She writes, "The Bible is in many ways alien and antagonistic to modern women's identity; yet, in other ways, it inspires and compels that identity."[30] This ambivalence grants womanist interpreters the freedom to read with and also against the biblical text in the service of abundant life beyond oppressive structures.

Womanist theologies of scripture lead us beyond a one-size-fits-all understanding of God. Furthermore, as one of the most marginalized and maligned people groups in the U.S., the advocacy for African American women's empowerment and cries for justice demand attention from all who would love their neighbor as themselves.

How Is This Still a Thing?

These theologies of scripture are but a sample of the breadth and richness you can find displayed by different Christian communities. It is far from exhaustive, and it fails to capture the nuance and range of interpretations within such demographic boundaries, but these are not the reasons I shared them with you. Rather, it is to show, as New Testament professor Brian Blount teaches us, that scripture is dynamic precisely because our interpersonal factors are in constant states of flux. The Bible is alive.[31] It bears witness to the Word of God that constantly subverts our simple, even simplistic, understandings of God. Scripture's vivacity is such that no passage of scripture can ever be wholly interpreted and no understanding of God is spared from critique.

To fail to listen to the neighbor whom God also loves is to fail to love at all.

The call for justice enunciated by liberation theologies of scripture raises an obvious question for the church. By way of analogy, British comedian and sociopolitical critic John Oliver, host of HBO's *Last Week Tonight*, often features a segment titled, "How Is This Still a Thing?" From Daylight Savings Time to Columbus Day, Oliver points a finger (usually the middle finger) at cultural oddities that linger in spite of being outmoded. Given the overwhelming testimony of scripture and the cogent theologies of scripture examined above, I have to ask the question: How can a singular, insulated understanding of God still be a thing?

All theologies are local theologies. All interpretations are contextual interpretations—and these declarations too are local and contextual for me. How can universal and absolute theologies of scripture still be a thing for those of us who are called to love our neighbors as ourselves? The church must respond that maybe it's still a thing because it's a tool of the oppressor that is us.

Even as all theologies and interpretations are contextual, one is not reducible to one's race, gender, sexuality, ethnicity, or favorite Teletubby—I'm a Tinky-Winky man myself. Rather, *myriad* factors shape a person's theology of scripture. To reduce readers according to gender, sexuality, race, etc. merely reinscribes another form of demographic reductionism (e.g., "Black women read the Bible like this," or "Gay men read the Bible like that").

Theologies and interpretive strategies are contextual. They are situated in particular communities at particular times.[32] To those who would insist upon a one-size-fits-all theology or interpretation sufficient to all times and places I say, these aren't the theologies you're looking for. *waves hand Obi-Wan Kenobi style* These are the theologies that teach us to love our neighbor in and through scripture.

Part II

Oppa Gangnam Style: The Bible as Rave

*A text is only a text if it hides from the first comer, from the
    first glance,
the law of its composition and the rule of its game.
A text remains, moreover, always imperceptible.*
                                            — JACQUES DERRIDA[1]

Loving our neighbor is not enough. Jesus also calls us to love God
with all of our being—heart, soul, mind, and strength. Not only
has God gifted us with others-as-neighbors to guide us on our
path to such love, God has also chosen to reveal Godself to us in
and through the Bible. But, as our engagement with cultural interpretations and liberation theologies of scripture has made abundantly clear, we are incapable of interpreting scripture in a vacuum.
If we really want to love God *in* scripture, then how we approach
the Word therein makes all the difference.

For those with eyes to see and ears to hear, the Bible is anything but a vapid container of theological truths. I would argue that scripture bears much in common with the contemporary hit, "Gangnam Style." Don't laugh. I'm serious. Of course you know the song, which is performed by South Korean pop musician Psy. You probably know the dance, too. In December 2014, the Internet announced that the song had broken the YouTube counter at 2,147,647 views! There is no denying that Gangnam style has gone viral; but the question remains: Has the Bible caught it?

Gangnam refers to the most affluent district in Seoul, South Korea, noted for its posh cultural ethos (think Beverly Hills). Psy explains that the Gangnam lifestyle is marked by excessiveness—clothes, looks, lifestyle, the whole shebang. In South Korea, Gangnam style is slang for cultural extravagance. It is similar in meaning to the American term, *swagger.*

The Word of God made known to us in scripture exudes something like Gangnam style. The Bible's got mad swagger, yo! Why? Because in it the Word speaks to us, calling us to abide in God. We could do worse than to see the Bible as an all-night dance party—a rave—that draws readers in with its melodious rhythms and sublime beats. Holy Scripture is anything but boring. It's not stagnant. It's alive. Scripture possesses an innate quality that can entrance, delight, and overpower the reader with its many ways of meaning. Such is the power of the Word.

Switching metaphors, the Bible is not a bland, meat 'n potatoes dish that sustains the body while evoking little pleasure. Rather, the Bible is a bacon-wrapped date stuffed with goat cheese and drizzled with a wasabi-balsamic reduction. Even as biblical texts pat you comfortingly on the shoulder, they kick you in the teeth. Mmmm, bacon.

So, here's the thing. The Bible is a collection of texts. We have to acknowledge its textuality so that we can embrace what God is up to in our reading of scripture. Texts, by nature, are open to multiple interpretations. They *do* things. Unfortunately, the last couple hundred years of biblical interpretation have been like that one time when you were twerking wantonly to Nicki Minaj at your kick-ass house party and your parents came home and forced everyone out. Mainstream biblical scholarship and theology force conformity and establish decorum for biblical interpretation. Talk about a buzzkill.

I don't know what your Sunday school experiences have been like, but mine have had little in common with a rave. Hardly have I read a Bible commentator and thought, "Damn, she's got swagger!" I rarely read theology and start to bob my head to that oh-so-catchy tune "Gangnam Style." *busts out best Psy dance moves* You know you like that!

What if we could change our approach to the Bible? What if we could make biblical interpretation exciting, life-giving? That's what I'm fittin' to learn you. Y'all ready?

Hey, you know what's exciting? Love is exciting. It stirs something inside you. It draws something out of you that you might not have even known you had. If your experience with the Bible is humdrum, if it feels like just another action item on your to-do list, you've got to ask yourself why. Is this what it feels like to be a Christ-follower—slogging through Leviticus? If you've lost that lovin' feeling, then let's go find it. Don't worry. I'll help you.

My experience with scripture has shown me that the Bible can absolutely lead you to love God and the world God loves more deeply. The first thing you've got to do is embrace the strangeness of the Word. This can only happen if you embrace the Bible's textuality. Words are slippery suckers. They mean all kinds of ways. Through them God speaks to us, but its ways of speaking are weird. If we want to love God in scripture then we must embrace the Bible's oddness. We must listen to what the Word is trying to say to us *in* the words of scripture.

To help us listen more carefully and love God more fully in scripture I'm going to teach you about deconstruction. Don't be scared. Just think about it. Everything the Bible teaches us about

God, the world, and ourselves is *constructed* out of words. Words, like the languages that give them meaning, are constructs. Words aren't holy. To claim otherwise is tantamount to idolatry. But God is holy. We must not worship created things; but neither can we ignore the fact that God has elected such weak vessels to tell us that God loves us. The Word is in the words.

Deconstruction is kind of like a redneck rager, where anything is possible and nothing is out of bounds. It rocks so hard that the foundations seem to quake. I make no promises that you will like what you find in deconstruction, but I do promise this: it won't be dull. So come on, y'all. Crank up the Skynard, get a little shine in that red Solo cup, and get ready to go HAM.

Chapter Five

Beware the Kragle: The World of Deconstruction

*Writing is ever errant. Wandering between an Origin that
    never was and an
End that never is, writing has always already begun and never
    finally ends.*

— MARK C. TAYLOR[1]

Deconstruction is radically oriented to life. It's a kind of orientation that helps us participate in the fullness of life. Because deconstruction shares a bunk with Justice at camp Shalom, it offers a way of loving God and neighbor more fully in and through our engagement with Holy Scripture. Because we cannot get around the constructed nature of biblical texts, deconstruction is the best way to live into the Bible in its very materiality. This will be new to those of us who were reared by mainstream methods of biblical interpretation. But new doesn't have to mean scary.

How about a cartoon example? Cartoons aren't scary, most of 'em anyway (looking at you Neil Gaiman). The computer-animated adventure, *The Lego Movie*, centers on a run-of-the-mill construction worker named Emmet Brickowski. Though he's as far from a superhero as you could imagine, Emmet stumbles—literally—into contact with an object of cosmic importance called the Piece of Resistance. According to Lego prophecy, the person able to wield the Piece of Resistance would be "the Special," a person of messianic proportions able to thwart the evil aspirations of Lord Business, who plots to freeze the Lego world in place with a master weapon called the Kragle. *Mwua-ha-ha-ha!*

As the narrative unfolds, we discern the motivation behind Lord Business's sinister machinations. Lord Business lives his life by the assumption that the "proper" way to build anything (with Legos) is by following the instructions precisely. He despises the anarchic impulses of others who deviate from the prescribed building schematics. It turns out that the Kragle is a tube of Krazy Glue with some of the logo's letters rubbed off. #spoileralert Only by gluing all of the pieces in their "proper" place can Lord Business avert the chaos that ensues when so-called "master builders" deviate from the plan.

Reading the Bible—like playing with Legos—can be life-giving. It can open us up to new worlds, new possibilities. Scripture can draw us closer to God and neighbor, or, as we see with so-called Christian organizations spewing hate in the name of Jesus, scripture can be used to perpetrate all kinds of evil. Biblical meaning can't be glued down. The love of God and neighbor requires us to constantly reconsider how our understanding of biblical texts calls us to make love happen in our lives and relationships today.

In many ways, the plot of *The Lego Movie* gives us a window into contemporary approaches to scripture. You see, around the same time that the author was pronounced DOA, other thinkers—

other master builders of sorts—came to see "pieces of resistance" at work within, behind, and around the biblical text. By pointing out these destabilizing features at work within the biblical architecture, these philosophers and theologians opened new ways of seeing God's work in and through scripture. They uncovered fresh ways of thinking about how God works toward human flourishing through the Bible. These methods of reading texts, which we will see are less methods and more like *ways of seeing*, came to be called *deconstruction*.

Deconstruction, You Say?

Deconstruction is an antidote to biblical idolatry. It presents us with a way of engaging biblical texts attuned to what God might be saying to us today in the Bible. It helps us see how our human constructs for understanding God's agency and human responsibility can just as easily become obstacles to God's work to make all things new through the Spirit. That's the kicker, isn't it? What's new today for our cultures and contexts will be old tomorrow #newwine #oldwineskins #Mark2:22. Deconstruction is like a theological cistern that is ever churning, keeping the biblical waters from becoming stagnant. Or, to put it more theologically, deconstruction is an orientation to that which is *holy* in Holy Scripture.

The best way to begin to think about deconstruction is to think about the difference between Steven Seagal and Chuck Norris. While both men have made their fortunes kicking ass on the silver screen, there is a marked difference between *how* said ass-kicking takes place.

Steven Seagal displays his martial prowess in the art of aikido, in which he is a 7th-dan black belt (which means he's really, really good—don't let the ponytail fool you). Seagal's films notwithstanding, aikido is a peaceful art that aims to equip practitioners with means of defending themselves while also protecting their attacker from injury. In essence, aikido works by using an attacker's force against him; it's a way of joining one's energy with an attacker's energy in the means of self-defense.

Chuck Norris has mastered several martial arts. He is a black belt in karate and an 8th-degree black belt grand master in tae kwon do. If you watch Chuck Norris fight, he bests his opponents through speed, agility, and power. He blocks his opponents' attacks and greets them with his own counterattacks. Nothing says, "Let's be friends," like a roundhouse kick to the temple. #chucknorrisonlybleedsontheinside

Mainstream theologies of scripture fight like Chuck Norris. Biblical interpreters and theologians spar with one another, employing a swirl of warrants and rebuttals to counter alternative perspectives. Through a kind of theological "might makes right" mentality, such theologians attempt to beat one another, along with we who talk about God today, into submission.

Conversely, deconstruction works much like Steven Seagal's method of fighting. *Deconstruction is philosophical aikido.* It's a way of unifying one's interpretive energy with that of a text in order to destabilize, and eventually constrain, the idolatrous elements at work within, behind, or around biblical texts. Deconstruction does not meet force with force, but finds ways of reading *with* scripture, and then using the force of scripture—its internal logic, its historical commitments, its cultural assumptions—to de-center theological constructs. Like Steven Seagal, deconstruction destabilizes the governing logics that make texts possible.

Deconstruction is what happens when we see that there are elements at work within all acts of discourse—be they biblical, literary, historical, or cultural—that at once strengthen and weaken the discourse itself. If you want the technical definition, deconstructionist readings of scripture expose us to those elements in our theological thinking that end up working against God's liberative purposes in the world revealed in scripture.

The term *deconstruction* is not synonymous with *destruction*; in fact, we might even associate the latter with Chuck Norris. Destruction destroys stuff. And like our old pal Humpty Dumpty, once something is destroyed it cannot be put back together again. Theological deconstruction, because it is much more peaceful, much more subtle, opens a way—or better, finds an opening—toward theological reconstruction. Deconstruction arises out of a biblical text's "trembling"—a tremor, not an earthquake.[2] Deconstruction is a name for ways of looking at biblical texts that are savvy to the philosophical, sociopolitical, theological, etc. commitments that operate *within*, *behind*, and *around* them.

Circumcising Abraham: Deconstructing Scripture with the Apostle Paul

You don't have to look hard to find deconstruction at work. For those with eyes to see, it is happening in all texts at all times. Deconstruction is not something that we do to scripture. Deconstruction is something the Bible does to itself. Though he doesn't always get it right, one of the most exemplary "master builders" in Holy Scripture is the Apostle Paul. Arguably the clearest example of Paul's theological aikido is found in his letter to the Romans.

Romans is one of the most theologically sophisticated texts in all of scripture—it's the Grey Poupon of biblical condiments. It is not surprising, therefore, that traces of deconstruction are visible at every point. I want us to focus on what Paul does in chapter 4 with his deconstruction of the Abraham narrative, but I think it will be helpful first to see how he gets to this point in his epistle.

Romans opens with the customary how-to-dos you'd expect of a Greco-Roman letter. But then, right out of the gate, Paul gets to meddlin'. He writes in chapter 1, "I am under obligation to *both* Greeks *and* to barbarians, *both* to the wise *and* to the foolish" (v. 14). This might not sound all that radical to us today, but believe me it was for Paul's audience. Greco-Roman culture had a very strong sense of honor and obligation. Honor was reserved for one's superiors and social equals. And this was no trickle-down system. In Rome, honor flowed upward and shame flowed downward. For Paul to write to those in the capital of the empire and profess his obligation to "Barbarians" (a racial slur signifying all who did not speak Greek), Paul is subverting the honor/shame culture and racial bias from within that culture. That's deconstruction, baby!

Furthermore, in verse 14 Paul also deconstructs the Greco-Roman ideology around the wisdom-foolishness duality. You see, wisdom was a big deal for the Greeks—they invented the word "philosopher," after all, which means "lover of wisdom." You might also be interested to know that in Plato's model city, the rulers were not kings, but philosophers. Wisdom was to the Greeks as kitchy, thrift store fashion is for Macklemore. *sings, "I'm gonna pop some tags."* Paul upsets the simple opposition between the learned and those who are literally "without knowledge" by placing them together.

Paul continues his argument slyly, which is deconstruction's favorite style. He opens by bashing the Gentiles (non-Jews). By the end of chapter 1 Paul sounds like a media pundit on Fox News, hurling insult after insult at those "others" who are not like "us" in every conceivable way. But then, Paul yanks the string he's been weaving and the whole tapestry unravels. In chapter 2 he flips the argument to his fellow Jews. ("Therefore, you are without excuse.") Taking a page from the Hebrew prophets' playbook (see Amos 1–2), Paul drops the hammer on his own people, and this will structure Paul's theological rebuke for the next two chapters.

In chapter 4, Paul moves to a key point in the argument he has been building all along, namely, that God has shown Godself to be radically concerned for the world and that such ought to bolster our radical concern for one another—be they Greek or non-Greek, Gentile or Jews. Paul ended chapter 3 by establishing God's unbiased faithfulness displayed most fully in Jesus Christ as that which engenders our faithfulness and justice. Thus, Paul situates faithfulness as a kind of seed that germinates deconstruction of the Jew-Gentile duality.

In Rom. 4:3 and again in 4:9, Paul cites a key verse from Gen. 15:6, a verse that would be equally received by both Jews and Gentiles: "Abraham had faith in God and it was credited to him as righteousness." Paul goes on to note that Abraham's faithfulness can in no way be associated with circumcision, because Abraham was deemed faithful *prior* to his circumcision. Circumcision, following Paul's Abrahamic deconstruction, is *neither* of no consequence *nor* of utmost consequence.

Reading between the lines of Paul's epistle, we can't miss noting that the mark of circumcision or its lack was polarizing and divisive within the community of Roman Christ-followers. The "cut" of circumcision (not only in its exclusion of women) was entangled with the Law and God's covenant with Israel. Since circumcision, as the mark of God's covenant, started with Abraham, Paul goes to the source. By his close reading of Abraham's story as the foundational narrative for first-century Jewish belief and practice, Paul undercuts (yeah, that pun was intended) the Jew-Gentile division *from within* the very tradition that seemed to establish the division. That is deconstruction.

Faithfulness, that is, "walking in the way of faith" (4:12), is the God-given hinge that opens all who are in Christ to participate in God's righteousness. Because God credited righteousness to Abraham according to his abiding faith in God, God has made the impossible possible.[3] Faith for Paul is thus a kind of crack in the infrastructure of Jewish faith and practice: it is a crack that simultaneously causes all Jewish claims to ethnic superiority to tremble, and that makes an opening on the inside of God's election of Israel for those on the outside of the historical covenantal relationship. Deconstruction, in this instance, participates in the very justice and faithfulness that Abraham received and which is now available to all who are in Christ Jesus.

Radioactive Texts: The Trace of Deconstruction

Deconstruction happens. This is good news for we who are perusing a path of love toward God and neighbor. Deconstruction is another way of celebrating that scripture is alive. Because the meaning of biblical texts is not fixed, because its meaning is never reducible to its historical context or authorial intent, we must participate in the Bible's aliveness, which is to say, its deconstruction. Furthermore, because the Spirit of God is continually moving through Holy Scripture, even as the Spirit is moving through us in our particular contexts, we must stay on our toes, so to speak, ever alert to what God is saying to us today.

Scripture is holy to the extent that God reveals God's holiness, God's radical otherness, to us through its many pages. We may only claim that the Bible is Holy if it also sets *us* apart, makes *us* holy, so that we may participate in God's love and justice in the world. Staying alive to God in and through scripture is what keeps us oriented to love of God and neighbor.

Another way to think about deconstruction vis-à-vis biblical texts is by thinking about radioactivity. Radioactivity is essentially a process of decay. It is the process by which the nucleus of an unstable atom loses energy by emitting ionizing radiation. A material that spontaneously emits this kind of radiation is considered *radioactive*. Texts—all texts, by their very nature—are sort of radioactive in that their very constitution is unstable. *Texts already leak meaning.* They are always in the process of coming undone at their core.

There are two things that we need to understand in relation to the radioactivity of biblical texts. First, the words that make up the Bible are not holy the way that God is holy. Words are signs. They point beyond the mark they leave behind on a page to something that is not fully present in the words themselves. Words are constructed out of a necessary absence. Words are at once present to their writer and reader, but their presence betrays a necessary absence, a *trace* within, behind, or surrounding their use in texts. Words most certainly exist, but their being is complicated by language itself, which structures being and nonbeing, past and present, sameness and otherness, Jedi Masters and Sith Lords. At the same time, the significatory potential of words is ongoing, infinitely *deferred*. Even if these contradictions are difficult to grasp, they are essential for understanding how deconstruction bears upon theologies of scripture.

Second, every biblical interpretation has a half-life (to keep the chemistry metaphor going) of textual meaning. What this means is that a given biblical interpretation might be true and good for a certain community at a certain time, but as circumstances change such an interpretation begins to lose its truthfulness and goodness. Biblical meaning is relative because the God who speaks to us in and through scripture is in relationship with us. God shows God's power and love more clearly because scriptural meaning doesn't keep past its expiration date.

How to Become a Theological Master Builder

Deconstruction is not any *thing*. You can't put it on a shelf next to your ALF collectibles and, ahem, "tobacco" paraphernalia. Deconstruction is an event. It arises unexpectedly, beyond even the horizon of expectation. It's a gift in the truest sense.

Deconstruction arises within, behind, or around the boundaries—the interpretive horizons—of biblical texts. It transpires at those moments of rupture, where the text throws itself into doubt. Deconstruction *takes place*—it opens a space within our understanding of God (aka theology) beyond anything that we can think or imagine about God. Scripture may rightly be called *holy* inasmuch as it refuses to remain locked in systems of thought. Because God is holy, the Bible deconstructs itself.[4] This last sentence is key.

To say that the Bible deconstructs *itself* is to say that we have no control over it. Deconstruction is theological to the extent that it loves God more than anything that has ever been said about God. The spirit of deconstruction is evident throughout church history. It arises whenever women and men bear witness to God's justice beyond human conceptualizations of justice. It both facilitates and participates in the dynamic energies of love of God and neighbor.

Deconstruction is not exactly a theological *method*, which would give us the sense that we can wield it, employ it for our predetermined ends. It's better to understand deconstruction as a theological *attitude, sensibility,* or *way of seeing* that is intentional with regard to the constructed nature of the biblical text. Deconstruction helps us understand how the architecture of even biblical texts is always already coming undone by the very measures we employ to build them up.[5] If deconstruction *is* anything, it's a way of seeing theologically.

May the Odds Be Ever in Your Favor: The Hunger Games of (Biblical) Interpretation

*In seeing that it is the fact of God's voice and not its particular
    content that matters,*
*the human imagination behind the scriptures gains control of
    the content of God's speech*
and in doing so regains its voice.

— ELAINE SCARRY[1]

Scripture is odd, and deconstruction offers a way of embracing its oddness. Deconstruction opens us up to the Word by helping us to engage critically the textual nature of the biblical text. Unfortunately, if there's one thing we can say for certain about Western

Christianity it's that it's not a fan of weird. Modernity in particular has aided and abetted the incarceration of the Bible's inherent strangeness, and deconstruction works to help us retrieve that feeling of dis-ease with the Bible that so many of us have been trained to ignore. If understanding texts is a kind of game, then the history of biblical interpretation is like *The Hunger Games.*

Suzanne Collins's international best-selling book trilogy, *The Hunger Games,* centers around an annual gladiatorial-style competition in which residents of the twelve districts must offer up a male and female child, or "tribute," to fight to the death in a competition that is equal parts death match and wilderness survival: think *Mad Max* meets *Survivor. The Hunger Games* is set in a post-apocalyptic society marked by privation for many and abundance for few. Sound familiar? I'm looking at you, 1 percenters. #occupy-wallstreet #occupytheBible

The Hunger Games are hosted by the Capital, the powerful minority marked by a decadence that makes Gangnam-style fashion look like the haute couture of *Duck Dynasty.* Throughout the trilogy, a phrase is often uttered, both to contestants and potential contestants of the Games: "May the Odds Be Ever in Your Favor."

Upon careful scrutiny—a kind of deconstructive reading—of this platitude, we may discern what is also at stake for those of us who seek a way to love God with our whole being and our neighbors as ourselves in and through scripture. In the very real hunger games of biblical interpretation we must fully understand what it means to pursue a Wor(l)d from the Lord that does not favor only one kind of reader, one kind of Christian.

May the odds be ever in your *favor.*

Mainstream methods of biblical interpretation produce interpretations that favor that group of people performing the interpretation. This has always been the case. Historically, the gatekeepers of biblical meaning have mostly been white males. They/we have tended to favor interpretations that maintain their/our dominance, no matter how magnanimous these interpretations may seem.

Following from a certain mode of engaging biblical texts, a certain deconstruction, biblical interpreters have uncovered biblical meanings that do not favor only one, select demographic. Because the Word of God is not constrained by the biblical text, but is always springing forth from scripture toward abundant life, toward the World of God, we're free to participate in those meanings in our own lives. Deconstructive readings of scripture expose us to the holy dynamism manifested in and through scripture.

Let's keep going.

May the *odds* be ever in your favor.

The plural noun *odds* is semantically rich. On one level, the word points to conditions of favorability, to likelihood, to chance. As a noun, it points to the ratio between the amounts staked and the probability expected of the outcome (*the odds of winning*). #allin

On another level, the word *odd* functions as an adjective, meaning *one who is different*, who doesn't conform to prescribed norms or conventions (e.g., "The neighbors thought him very *odd*."). Here the word is synonymous with the adjective *strange*. More often than not, the word *odd* is wielded by those in power. Power is knowledge, and the ones in control of discourse and society get to determine that which deviates from the "norm," that which is *odd*; they get to decide who the "odd ones" are. This is ludicrous. We are all odd according to cultural standards different from our own.

If deconstruction is anything, it is odd. It bets against the house, not because it aims to win, but because it knows that the game is already rigged. Even by losing, it wins. At the same time, deconstruction is odd to the extent that it operates in tension with the structural flow. Again, this is not a negative operation; rather, it is one that participates in the internal, underlying, and/or surrounding regimes of knowledge that bolster an argument. Deconstruction, by its oddness, displays the instability of the system of thought itself. This book—this entire line of *Theology for the People* books—is *odd* inasmuch as it works with and subverts the so-called standards of academic publishing.

Since (at least) the early nineteenth to the third quarter of the twentieth century, the odds have ever been in the favor of those with power: Western, white, educated, heterosexual males. Following the death of the author and the emergence of deconstruction, several modes of biblical interpretation have arisen to challenge the hegemonic reign of mainstream methods of biblical interpretation. As with the various forms of cultural interpretations, such modes of engagement with the biblical text are much more fun to witness than to explain.

If You Build It They Will Come (Undone): Radical Readings of Scripture

Deconstructive approaches to scripture are just as diverse as contextual methods of interpretation—nearly as diverse as the people rendering such interpretations. It is false to say that there is one way of reading a scripture passage sensitive to its deconstruction. Rather, the readings emerging out of such radically diverse intellectual frameworks as poststructuralism and postcolonialism, eco-justice and queer theology, are both profuse and varied.[2]

In spite of the great diversity of these readings of scripture they each possess a common trait. It is this point of convergence that makes such readings so important and instructive for we who would seek to make love with scripture. Deconstructive modes of interpreting scripture share a certain radicality, that is, they expose themselves to the root (*radix*) of undecidability in play with every interpretation of scripture. Radical readings of scripture, each in their own way, recognize and even celebrate their own rootedness and rootlessness.

Radical readings of scripture, in spite of the myriad forms they take, are unified in their orientation to a certain dis-ease at work in texts and in the communities inspired by those texts. They attend to the textual, cultural, and ideological tenuousness of biblical texts and biblical interpretations, often destabilizing the hierarchies established and sustained by biblical texts. Such readings grate against interpretive efforts oriented toward unity and cohesion. Let's look at some examples.

Faltering at the Fault Line: Deconstructing the Tower of Babel

The tower of Babel narrative found in Gen. 11:1-9 is one of the most well-known stories in the Bible. This story serves as a kind of hinge for all of the primordial stories before it and the election of Abraham that follows after it. As feminist Hebrew Bible scholar Danna Nolan Fewell writes, "In biblical studies, Babel is rarely allowed to stand alone; rather, the story is seen to be both the crowning episode in the longer story of Genesis 1–11 and the transition into, indeed the necessity for, the call of Abraham in Genesis 12."[3] So, this text is kind of like that scene in *The Karate Kid* when Daniel-san thinks he's finished painting the fence when he's only just begun.

Fewell offers a feminist deconstructive reading of the Babel narrative by reading it against two dominant currents of interpretation in biblical studies. On the one hand, scholars have interpreted the tower of Babel narrative in relation to "the fall," where God forecloses on Adam and Eve's house and they are forced to move into that dodgy old trailer park that smells of cat pee and Camel Lights. Here the story is read to demonstrate humanity's insatiable drive to be like God, and the primeval "fall" of Babel is read as the setup for God's election of Abraham as the one through whom God would build a great nation (see Gen. 12:2-3). In short, Babel is seen to set the stage for God's redemption of the cosmos. Fewell labels this the "vertical reading," which regards the tower as a monument to human ingenuity in its quest to rival God.

On the other hand, scholars have interpreted the Babel narrative as God's way of "filling the earth" (see 1:28) and "tilling the

ground" (2:5). By this reading, God's response to the building project undertaken at Babel is not a punishment, but a reorientation,
a gentle push out of the nest so that humanity could fulfill God's
plan to copulate, cultivate, and care for the world—the 3-Cs, I call
them. Fewell labels this the "horizontal reading," which sees the
tower as a watchtower, a bulwark of the city designed to divide
insiders from outsiders.

After laying out these two traditional modes of interpreting
the Babel narrative, Fewell shows us her wicked aikido moves
through her feminist-deconstructionist reading, a reading that
makes the foundations of subsequent interpretive "towers" tremble. She reads the Babel narrative in accordance with both of
these traditions, tracing each reading's mode of foreshadowing
throughout the history of Israel. She follows the energy of these
two strands of interpretation, and then, once she's redirected each
reading's center of gravity, she makes her move. *Hadouken!*

At the "top of the tower," Fewell sees the hubris that gives rise
to violence and power, one in which masters command slaves to
build them a tower, a symbol of the latter's domination that will
eventually draw the exiles of Israel back to the city of Babylon.
Those at the "bottom of the tower," those who actually build the
tower, are enslaved by language and the concentration of power,
which she sees as a foreshadowing of Daniel's story. Fewell concludes, "When one considers those on both the top and bottom
of Babel, the scattering in Genesis 11 becomes ambivalent: It is a
punishment for the taskmaskers and yet an emancipation for the
enslaved and conscripted workers."[4]

Under Fewell's scrutiny this narrative shows us its own mul-
tivalence and ambivalence—like that time you were shroomin' in
Myrtle Beach and you thought that painting was just a bunch of
dots and then, *kaboom*, it's not a bunch of dots, but Jesus dressed
as John Wayne riding a dolphin hurtling toward the Death Star.
#goodtimes We learn from Fewell that the building of walls and
towers teeters between pain and imagination, between insiders

and outsiders. The efforts to restore to Israel a place and a name after exile comes at a price. This is a price borne by those on the bottom of Babel—the poor, the homeless, women, foreigners. The place of security and identity for those at the top of Babel relies on the insecurity and stripping of identity from those on the bottom. Babel is *both* and *always* vertical and horizontal.

Fewell's reading of Babel, like the tower itself, "scatters us in multiple directions."[5] It throws us off kilter. It makes us tremble along with the tower. Both the biblical text and the tower are always already coming undone, and Fewell's reading shows us how such a mode of reading may open up new ways of thinking about the biblical text as well as contemporary faith and practice.

The Humor of Subverting Identity: A Queer, Postcolonial Reading of Rahab

Hebrew Bible scholar Erin Runions opens her essay, "From Disgust to Humor: Rahab's Queer Affect," with a simple question: Why do so many Americans meet the topic of nonheteronormative sex with revulsion and abhorrence? The answer, she suggests, might just be because so many Americans have read the Bible. Adding to her critique, Runions points out that much of the disgust that maps onto biblical descriptions of sexuality is inextricable from racial bias.[6] Israel's history is one of hatin' all over other racial/ethnic groups, particularly the Canaanites.

In the story of Rahab, the Canaanite prostitute in Jericho whom we encounter in Joshua 2, Rahab hides from her king two Israelite spies. Through her surreptitious actions and negotiating prowess, Rahab saves both herself and her family in the conquest about to ensue. What is odd about this text, an oddness that Runions seizes upon, are the ways in which both Rahab and the text itself act in and against stereotypical identity markers: prostitute, Canaanite. Both designations are used throughout Hebrew scripture as terms of derision and abomination.

In Rahab's tale, we find neither critique of her profession, nor condemnation of her ethnic identity. In complete contrast, the prostitute/Canaanite—the quintessential other—becomes the *subject*, seizing control of her own story and upsetting all expectations like Thelma, or Louise.

In many ways, Runions's argument follows that of other prominent queer theorists. The term "Canaanite" functions similarly to the term "homosexual," in that both are used as identity markers employed to set the boundary-line between the supposed "insiders" (Israelites, heterosexuals) and "outsiders" (Canaanites, homosexuals).[7] From a postcolonial perspective, Runions also notes the ways in which Rahab subverts the efforts of the colonizers along with the imperial rule to which she is also subjected.

Runions's essay showcases the many ways in which a deconstructive approach or sensibility opens fresh ways of seeing the biblical text. One of the layers of investigation is at that of redaction, which attends closely to the ways in which the particular copy we have in our Bibles was pieced together over the centuries in service of ideological and theological aims. Such layers of redaction—editing, amending, elaborations—expose the text to new interpretations and insights.

For instance, many scholars believe that Rahab's confession of faith (vv. 9-14) and the spies' conditions of protection (vv. 17-21) were later elaborations intended to bring this narrative more in line with later ideological and theological sensibilities. So, at the level of textual construction, the earlier version of the story is believed to have consisted of 2:1-8, 15-16, and 22-23, namely, Rahab's handling of both the Israelite spies and the king, which precipitated the spies' safe retreat.

On the level of narrative affect, the story supports a transgressive interpretation. First, the spies don't exactly follow Joshua's command to "go see the land" (v. 1), for in the very same breath the narrator tells us that the spies veer off mission and "bed down" in the home of a prostitute. "One can almost hear the wink and the nod" of the narrator.[8] It's gettin' spicy!

Next, Rahab hides the Israelite spies/customers from the investigations prompted by the Canaanite king. You don't have to stretch to imagine the comedic commotion caused by two men in various states of undress being forced to hide in a hot, scratchy flaxen roof. Rahab then spins a yarn for the inquisitive guards who (somehow) got wind of the spies' presence. It is worth noting that the spies' imagined intention behind visiting Rahab's brothel was thwarted when she forces them to retreat (v. 8: "before the spies bedded down"). Runions notes that Rahab actually succeeds in utterly foiling both the spies' military orders ("to go and look") and their personal desires vis-à-vis Rahab ("to go and enter"). She makes the spies look like buffoons.

Runions argues convincingly that the story's humor works to subvert disgust. She writes, "The usual object of disgust (the Canaanite)—normally repelled by the subject (the Israelite, or the reader so identified)—becomes the subject (the Canaanite Rahab) repelling the object (the Israelite spies). Combined with a positive revaluation of the new subject, this reversal is funny."[9] The humor of the story causes the typical feeling of disgust to lose its stickiness.

Rahab transgresses societal structures by leaning fully into her identity among her people (as a prostitute) and her racial difference among the Israelite spies (as a Canaanite). In other words, there are many other ways that Rahab could have handled things. She could have called her king's army right to where the spies were hidden. She could have fled the city with the spies to save herself. She could have let the spies depart under a false pretense of her complicity and then alerted the king to prepare a surprise counterattack. She did none of these things.

Instead, Rahab embodies a certain *oddness*, an oddness that disrupts the biblical text from within. Like queer and postcolonial theories, Rahab's transgressiveness opens onto a kind of subversiveness. Said differently, she leans fully into her own oddness and thereby challenges simplistic notions of insider/outsider and simple labels to her own identity. Runions concludes, "Rahab, in her almost-but-not-quite hybridity—between the city and the gate, text and redaction, Canaanite and Israelite—is well positioned to make the jokes that upset the status quo, even while perhaps seeming uncomfortably to maintain it."[10] The ambiguities of this text are such that we ought not claim Rahab as the poster girl for heteronormative or colonial liberation. Rather, by a certain sense of humor, we see how Rahab queers her textual identity, as well as the reader's.

Dirty Water? A Discursive Reading of Metaphor in John's Gospel

New Testament scholar Stephen Moore draws upon a number of critical tools (poststructural, discursive, postcolonial, and queer theories, to name a few) in his investigations of biblical texts. His reading of the Woman at the Well narrative in John 4:7-15 showcases a mode of interpretation that destabilizes the discursive logic of scripture, opening new interpretations.[11]

To begin, Moore observes that one of the most salient points that feminist and traditional interpretations of the Well narrative have failed to notice is the power differential that remains in place *through* Jesus' interaction with the Samaritan woman. In other words, Jesus retains a position of superiority, maintaining his privileged role as *the dispenser of knowledge*.

Thus, as long as this power dynamic prevails, Jesus' supposed "boundary-breaking" activity (a Jewish man speaking to a Samaritan woman) maintains the very boundaries he is purported to deconstruct. Moore then asks some deconstructive questions: "But what if the Samaritan woman were found to be the more enlightened partner in the dialogue from the outset? What if her insight were found to exceed that of Jesus all along? Impossible? Not at all, as I hope to show."[12] And show us he does.

To show how the supposedly *pure* and *living water* that Jesus offers is better than the *profane* water in the well, Moore follows this water downstream, showcasing its reappearance in chapters 7 and 19 of John's Gospel.

In John chapter 7, on the last day of the Feast of Tabernacles, Jesus speaks again of such supramundane water. In 7:38, Jesus says, "Out of his heart shall flow rivers of living water." Whose heart, exactly? Jesus told the Samaritan women that those who drink the water that he, Jesus, gives them will themselves flow with rivers of living water (4:14). And yet in 4:10, Jesus gestures to himself as the *source* of the living water.

Which is it?

The believer is more than a mere receptacle for surplus water. She is more than an overflow; rather, she is a channel, or conduit, in her own right. Jesus cites scripture in John 7:38 to bolster his argument that it is he who is the source of living water ("As the scripture has said, 'Out of the believer's heart shall flow rivers of living water'"). But wait a minute, John's Jesus seems to be inadvertently creating a rival water source.[13] Is the water from Jesus or the believer?

Moore also draws our attention to another water source in John's Gospel. In John 19:28, Jesus, hanging on the cross, says, "I thirst." So, here the living water cries out for mundane water. What then is the referent of this request? Is Jesus seeking literal water or, figuratively, does he desire another kind of water, a water that triggers a more consuming thirst? The soldiers honor Jesus' request by giving him "sour wine" (cf. Ps. 69:22). Thus, with a final drink of this *sour wine*, this impure water, Jesus shouts, "It is finished," and then, the narrator laments, Jesus "gave up his spirit" (John 19:30). Moore draws our attention to the impurity of the living water/spiritual metaphor, now muddled and murky through its exposure to well water and watered-down wine. He ends by noting that the satiation of Jesus' *physical* thirst conditions the proleptic yielding up of that which is intended to satiate the *spiritual* thirst of the believer, namely, the Holy Spirit.

At the Samaritan well, water is neither simply material and literal, since it is symbolic, nor is it fully spiritual and figurative, since it is physical. Moore concludes, "Literality and figurality intermingle in the flow from Jesus' side, each contaminating the other, which is to say that we cannot keep the literal clearly separate from the figurative in the end."[14] Such a reading opens us up to the internal tensions of scripture, and thereby calls for deeper reflection.

To Volunteer as Tribute

Both *The Hunger Games* and the history of biblical interpretation teach us that the odds are *never* in the favor of those who are on the margins of (theological) power. We can talk and even preach that the liberating power of God is available to all; however, when only certain interpretations are deemed admissible, that which one is given theologically is taken away interpretively. How you interpret scripture manifests your theology of scripture. Likewise, how you understand God's agency in the world of the text will shape how you adjudicate the text's meaningfulness. Theology and interpretation are inseparable.

In the Hunger Games of biblical interpretation, men and women who find themselves on the margins of theological/interpretive power are a lot like the tributes in Suzanne Collins's narrative universe. Historically, they are the children (read: most vulnerable and least equipped) who must be sacrificed in order to bolster the (interpretive) monopoly of the Capital (read: white, Western, heterosexual men).

One of the most powerful elements in *The Hunger Games* is that the story's protagonist, a teenage girl named Katniss Everdeen, was *not* selected to fight in the Hunger Games. The odds were in her favor that day, but not for Katniss's little sister. Katniss volunteered as tribute. She took her sister's place, thereby willingly subjecting herself to the risks germane to the Games. This ought to quicken we who have received favor by the reigning powers and principalities on account of our race, gender, sexuality, etc. to fight for and alongside those who find themselves on the underside of such systems. *lifts three-fingers in a solidarity salute*

Chapter Seven

Don't Win the Game. Change It: Radical Theologies of Scripture

A discourse can poison, surround, close off, and imprison,
or it can liberate, cure, nourish, and fecundate. It is rarely
neutral.

— LUCE IRIGARAY[1]

The greatest hit series on television right now is the music drama *Empire*, with its first season finale reaching the highest number of viewers of any show in the last five years. The show centers on the work and relationships of entertainment mogul Lucious Lyon, his ex-wife Cookie, and their three grown sons who all participate in various ways in the family hip-hop empire.

In one episode, Lucious's youngest son, Hakeem, pitches a rap song to his father around the boardroom at Empire Entertainment. His father immediately loves his son's song, seeing in it both the income potential for the family and the means to his favorite son's rise to stardom. At the apogee of his pitch Hakeem says, "I don't wanna win the game. I wanna change it." With these final words he wins his father's unequivocal endorsement.

Many who have come to understand the "rules" of theological interpretations of scripture are not that different from *Empire's* Hakeem. Such thinkers realize that the so-called "rules" of "proper" interpretation have been established to benefit a certain kind of reader: the white, Western, educated, affluent, heterosexual male. (FADE IN: Ghostly image approaches with George W. Bush's head on Sylvester Stallone's body. *MWAHAHA-HAHAHAHAHA!* Everybody freaking run!) Such intellectual accommodations privilege one mode of thinking, thereby marginalizing others.

These alternative kinds of theologies of scripture I'm talking about arise out of a kind of *subversion*—not an outright rejection, which would still be playing by the "rules of the game," as it were. Such alternative theologies undermine the intellectual assumptions and ideological foundations that bolster mainstream modes of biblical interpretation. A kind of catch-all label for such theologies of scripture is encapsulated by the modifier *radical*.[2]

Hybrid Readings: Postcolonial Theologies of Scripture

Postcolonial theologies of scripture highlight the Bible's sociopolitical ambivalence. What postcolonial biblical criticism does, writes Sri Lankan biblical scholar R. S. Sugirtharajah, is "to make this ambivalence and paradox clear and visible."[3] Postcolonial theologies of scripture teach us that the Bible has functioned simultaneously as the Word of God *and* the word of empire. They remind us that scripture has been used to justify all sorts of imperialistic advances. After all, the Bible provided the theological rationale for colonialism, which was theologically dubious—dubious the same way that Lehman Brothers is in terms of fiscal responsibility, or the way that Justin Bieber is in terms of musicality.[4]

Let us not for one second look at the history of colonial oppression from our twenty-first-century American context, and say to ourselves, "Man, those folks way back when were a bunch of tools. I'm glad we aren't like that today." Tut. Tut. I say we are *exactly* like that today.

America is plagued by the disease of Special Snowflake Syndrome. This is a contracted condition that afflicts the ego; it's where we believe ourselves to be utterly unique and better than everyone else. Thank God we have the Apostle Tyler Durden to set us straight: "You are not special. You are not a beautiful or unique snowflake. You're the same decaying organic matter as everything else." Umm. Hold on. That can't be right. *checks notes* Oh. Wrong sermon. The Apostle *Paul* sets us straight: "There is no distinction; all of us have sinned and fall short of God's glory" (Rom. 3:22-3). My bad.

Postcolonial theologies of scripture attend critically to the structures of power, systems of dominance, and embedded ideologies at work *within* scripture. Jesus' entire life and ministry transpired under imperial rule, after all. Botswanan feminist biblical scholar Musa Dube insists that we must ask the hard questions as to "why biblical texts endorsed unequal power distribution along geographical and racial differences; why, in the wake of political independence, power has remained unequally distributed; and how to read for empowering the disempowered areas and races or creating a better system."[5] Through such questions, postcolonial theologies of scripture negotiate alternative ways of being for colonized and previously colonized persons, seeking new avenues for social transformation that recognize and validate the perspectives of marginalized peoples, cultures, and identities.

Attending to the complexity of centuries of colonial oppression, much of which rests upon a *biblical* foundation, postcolonial theologies of scripture do not merely deny colonial ideologies and modes of biblical interpretation. They are much too radical for that. Rather, inasmuch as such theologians recognize the many striations of difference ingrained in personal and communal identities, they make room for a multiplicity of responses, hoping to achieve a reciprocal exchange of perspectives from all voices. Postcolonial theologies of scripture seek above all *emancipation* and *authenticity* for all marginalized or oppressed persons. Thus, it engages issues of nationality, culture, race, gender, economic status, and sexuality.

At their core, postcolonial theologies of scripture are pragmatic, recognizing that meaning arises out of one's context to inspire awareness, critical dialogue, and integration of ideas. The primary goals of postcolonial theologies of scripture are to critique hegemonic theological constructions that make absolutist or totalitarian claims, and to provide legitimacy for alternative theological views and biblical interpretations. These goals have real-world implications.

Postcolonial theologies of scripture place the colonized "other" at the center of theological interpretation. They engage God's Word apart from the "idolatry of identity," that is, by refusing to assign an "essential sameness" to biblical interpreters, but instead such theologies highlight the connections between persons, their environments, and the rest of the world.[6]

This reorientation of (previously) colonized persons from the margins to the center of biblical meaning-making contributes to postcolonial liberationist readings of Holy Scripture.[7] This helps us all see that the so-called "natives" living under colonial oppression were not merely hapless recipients of the "white man's book," but have been and continue to be *active* producers of interpretation.

But this reorientation is not simple. Postcolonial feminist theologian Kwok Pui-lan explains, "The most important contribution of postcolonial feminist theology will be to reconceptualize the relation of theology and empire through the multiple lenses of gender, race, class, sexuality, religion, and so forth."[8] Postcolonial theologies of scripture and their accompanying ways of enlivening biblical interpretation subvert, challenge, and reconceptualize the underlying ideologies of theology and empire, thereby exposing the roots of oppression to the drill of deconstruction. *Bzzzt. Bzzzt.*

Over the Rainbow: Queer Theologies of Scripture

In some circles, the word *queer* is still an offensive, even derisive term. However, many biblical and theological scholars have reclaimed this term to signify a theoretical framework—a "critical sensibility more than a methodology"—that embraces its own oddities and particularity. Queer theory brings a primal sense of otherness to our consciousness.[9] It provokes wild, risky, even dangerous engagements with the biblical text. It sees God's Word not as a placid, pristine pond of theological truths, but as a tsunami of theological possibilities.

In queer theory, the word *queer* is a descriptor for those who define themselves outside the "normal" mode of sexual expression (heterosexual) or gender identity (cisgender). By this use of the term, queer is synonymous with Lesbian, Gay, Bisexual, Transgender, Intersex, etc. Thus, according to this usage, *queer* theologies of scripture would signify understandings of God's agency in and through scripture from people in these groups. Accordingly, the *queer* in queer theology falls in line with other contextualized interpretations like those we have examined above (feminist, African American, etc.).

But queer theology is also "radically different from gay and lesbian theology."[10] Queer theory supports queer theologies of scripture, not by fighting for a space for LGBTI persons to interpret scripture in light of their lived realities, but, on a deeper level, in challenging the discursive norms that *structure* such conditions of knowledge, thereby liberating *everyone* from contemporary constructions of sexuality and gender. In other words, to claim the word *queer* is to assert a specific position of knowledge, a particular frame of viewing the world, and the biblical text.

Queer theologies of scripture do (at least) three things vis-à-vis the biblical text: they challenge dualistic constructions of reality; they are oriented to concrete practices of liberation; and they bask in the glow of Divine excess.

First and foremost, queer theologies of scripture challenge dualities. Male/female, orthodox/heterodox, gay/straight, Donald Trump/all human beings who are not Donald Trump—these dualities are used to reduce people to a simple label that is destabilized by queer theology.

Queer theologies of scripture unsettle dualistic ideologies by queering the *logic* of the biblical witness. For instance, theologian Patrick Cheng employs a Jesus-inspired, incarnational theology of love to upset traditional modes of theological thought. He writes, "Ultimately, God's coming out is an act of radical love because, like the coming out experience for LGBT people, it results in the dissolving of existing boundaries" (e.g., divine/human; powerful/weak; knowing/unknowing).[11] When God comes out of the closet we have to wonder who built the closet in the first place.

Second, queer theologies of scripture see God at work in the liberation of human and nonhumans (e.g., creation) through particular, concrete manifestations of liberation practices. Elizabeth Stuart puts it as clearly as it can be found: "This is the nature of queer theology—liberation." She continues, "Queer Christians are not interested in abstract, universal doctrines." The gospels provide queer Christians with the "dangerous memory of a subjugated knowledge of a God who stands in solidarity with the oppressed."[12] A theology that supports the status quo has no place among queer theologies of scripture—in fact, such are a #2 pencil to the neck of such theologies, not *literally* of course; move on, there's nothing to see here.

Third, queer theologies of scripture seek to participate in the superabundance of meaning that scripture exhibits. Contextual theologian Marcella Althaus-Reid articulates a theology of scripture in such a radical vein. By setting the many valves of difference wide open rather than closing them down to a trickle, Althaus-Reid and other queer theologians offer readings of scripture that are the theological equivalent of the Super Soaker Monster XL, the dual-nozzled beast of destruction that makes all others look like mini squirt guns. Their readings of scripture bring a battery of tools to the task of interpretation, offering up the text to ever-new possibilities.

Queer theologies of scripture offer these three guiding threads into the jungle of biblical interpretation. #welcometothejungle Such readings identify problematic gender, sexual, and theological stereotypes at work both *within* and *through* Holy Scripture. It is not just about reading from a particular sociopolitical location. Queer theologies subvert traditional interpretations and normative approaches to the Bible and to Western paradigms of thought.

What Would Jesus Deconstruct? Poststructural Theologies of Scripture

Poststructural theologies of scripture arise out of deconstruction. This is the most popular of deconstruction's love babies—it's the Kim Kardashian of biblical interpretation, so popular that sometimes we can hardly remember the names of its sisters. Poststructural theologies of scripture work *in* and *against* a certain "structural blindness" that harbors the "absolute secret" of biblical meaning.[13] Such theologies see God as radically beyond any meaning we might attach to God.

You see, the situation of the thoughtful Christian before the Word of God structures a double-bind. She is driven by her desire for God, to know God more fully, and yet this desire is met with resistance in the biblical texts that simultaneously reveal God and reveal God's inaccessibility.

Poststructural theologies of scripture recognize that behind every theological construction, indeed *in* every theological construction, lies a truth exceeding construction, a truth that structures the conditions of im-possibility for said construction. In his book *What Would Jesus Deconstruct?*, poststructural philosopher and oftentimes theologian John Caputo observes that always already at work within the *same*, the *familiar*, the *safe*, bursts the *event* of the other, of the *coming of the other*, which makes the same, the familiar, and the safe tremble and reconfigure.[14] In other words, the Word of God cannot be contained or constrained by the words of scripture.

Poststructural theologies of scripture hold that because language, as well as certain psychic and political commitments, preexists theological articulation, those structures and ideologies cannot be ignored. *Before theology speaks, philosophy has already spoken.*

The ways of interpreting scripture that accompany poststructural theologies of scripture are equally radical. Caputo identifies such a mode of interpretation as a "hermeneutics of the kingdom." This is a deconstructive mode of interpretation forever open to *the impossible*. For Caputo, it is a form of prayer.

Another way of talking about the radical interpretations opened by poststructural theologies of scripture is through the language of poetics. Philosopher Richard Kearney also writes about the kingdom of God as an image that tethers the future with the past, the (biblical) tradition with the hope yet to be realized. Such a kingdom orientation leads to an interpretive poetics, which Kearney describes as "an event of creative imagination," where imagination and reality make and remake each other.[15]

Caputo writes that a poetics—a theopoetics—that participates in kingdom modes of reading and talking about scripture is "evocative and provocative." He commends a way of approaching God that does not lock God down in structures of meaning, even creedal structures. It is a way that is radically open to what God *may* be up to in the present.

Poststructural theologies of scripture open a path toward biblical interpretations that exceed the bounds of scripture as a *thing* in the world, that is, an object with its own independent existence. Radical interpretations are *radical* inasmuch as they recognize the Word beyond linguistic structures, superseding human logic. A fancy-pants way of saying this is that such interpretations participate in the articulation of *the event*. For Caputo and others, *the event* points to a spatio-temporal occurrence *within* whatever we think we mean when we employ signifiers like God, Word, etc. The event harbored in the name "God" cannot be foreseen or forestalled. It can only be witnessed in all of its profundity.

Like God's radical self-emptying in the person of Jesus and mighty display of powerlessness on the cross, interpretations oriented toward God's kingdom manifest a "weak force." As Caputo explains, "In a *poetics* of the impossible, we mean to pose the possibility of something life-transforming, not to report how an omnipotent being intervenes upon natures' regularities and bends them to its infinite will."[16] In other words, interpretation is called to participate in the weakness of God, to hold on to our interpretations loosely. Only then are we reading the Bible in the mode of faith—knowing beyond knowledge and seeing beyond sight.

The Body of God: Ecotheologies of Scripture

A final radical theology of scripture to consider is that of ecotheology. Ecotheology is a form of constructive theology that tethers reflection on God to the created order, and particularly to environmental concerns.

Let's get this out right up front: Christianity in general, and literalist interpretations of scripture in particular, is culpable for the present ecological crisis. Certain interpretations of the Bible, particularly what it means to *have dominion* over the earth (Gen. 1:26-8), whether to *cultivate* and *care* for it, or *subdue* and *dominate* it, have been used to facilitate such deplorable practices as mountaintop removal, deforestation, wanton burning of fossil fuels, and the pollution of water sources.

This is both unacceptable and theologically untenable. Theologian John Cobb, one of the earliest proponents of "greening" the theological academy, writes unequivocally, "The restriction of attention to human beings, abstracted from their environment, cannot be found in the Jewish scriptures or the teachings of Jesus."[17] Indeed, *the land* is a central motif throughout scripture, and at no point are human beings excluded from the rest of creation. The story of redemption itself is linked to the renewal of nature, as we see in Rev. 21:5 when the resurrected Christ proclaims that he is making *all things* new.

Arguably the most tireless and unflinching advocate for ecotheologies of and beyond scripture is Sallie McFague. She urges us to think of the world as God's very body, which she hastens to add is "only one model, but one that is neglected, essential, illuminating and helpful both to Christian doctrinal reformulation and to planetary well-being." By this metaphor, which finds ample support in scripture, we are empowered to "meet God in and through the world, if we are ever to meet God. God is not out there or back there or yet to be, but hidden in the most ordinary things of our ordinary lives." She continues, "If we cannot find the transcendent *in* the world, in its beauty and its suffering, then for us bodily, earthy creatures it is probably not to be found at all."[18]

Ecotheologies of scripture help us see God in new ways, ways that are radically different than traditional theological constructions. Alirio Cáceres Aguirre urges that we should supplement our notion of God as father, mother, champion, etc. and to think also of God as *ecosystem*. This would constitute an inversion, whereby eco-theology becomes theo-ecology. More specifically, Aguirre encourages us to understand God as an "ecosystem of love, as an infinite network of loving relationships."[19] This is not without biblical warrant, for Paul himself described God to the people of Athens as the One "in whom we live and move and have our being" (Acts 17:28-29). Such a theology offers much for us to ponder.

Ecotheologies of scripture offer not only new understandings of God, but also of ourselves in relation to God through scripture and nature. McFague argues convincingly that contemporary persons are faced with two models of being in the world: the organic model and the mechanical model. The organic model sees the individual as part of a biological and cosmic community of living beings and the systems that support them. The mechanical model separates human beings from one another and from the created order, claiming that the forces that control and support life do not pertain to us or shape our destinies.[20]

Ecological ways of interpreting scripture participate in this central theological vision of ecotheology, and it has taken two separate though overlapping courses in biblical studies. On the one hand, ecologically oriented biblical scholars have sought to defend Christianity against the accusations of secular critics that the Bible is inherently human-centered, and thus apathetic to environmental concerns. On the other hand, biblical scholars have searched the scriptures for ecological wisdom capable of guiding faith and practice (*The Green Bible* is an example).

Ecological interpretation also manifests itself in a more radical strain of ecotheology. Such an approach is modeled by the Earth Bible project curated by Norman Habel. The Earth Bible project recognizes that the biblical texts were written by humans for humans and is preoccupied with human concerns. Thus, the Earth Bible team slaps the taste out of the mouths of exclusively human-centered interpretations of scripture. They call this "ecojustice," which regards Earth as a *subject* rather than an object in the text, and which is sensitive to the ways in which Earth is treated unjustly in the text.[21] In short, like liberation theologies, an ecojustice interpretation attends to the marginalized voice of Earth, and like other radical theologies of scripture, it challenges the foundational assumptions of mainstream theologies and modes of interpretation.

Reading Again, Differently

Christianity has been compared to DDT. The latter "destroys parasites, carriers of disease," while the former "roots out heresy, natural impulses, and evil."[22] Is this the best we can offer the world? I think not. Radical theologies of scripture, which have emerged out of the changes and conflicts of the past several decades, offer us a vision for Christianity that is oriented toward abundant life, not disease.

Is it possible for us to imagine a new way of being with God and neighbor, a way inspired by scripture? I believe there is, and I believe that this brief survey of radical theologies of scripture offer ways toward this destination—nay, not a destination, but a journey into a strange land inaugurated by Jesus Christ. Can we exhibit the faith of Abraham? Can we heed such a calling?

Given the history of Christian oppression, marked as it is by the sordid details of colonialism, heterosexism, fundamentalism, and anti-environmentalism, embarking on such a path might seem impossible. But we lean into Jesus' words that with God all things are possible (Mark 10:27). Radical theologies of scripture and their concomitant interpretive strategies allow us to travel the old paths of biblical interpretation afresh. They offer a third way beyond the extremes of dogmatic theism and militant atheism. Kearney calls such an approach "anatheism."

Anatheism is a way of thinking about God in our postmodern, postcolonial, post-Christian world equipped with a "new acoustic attuned to the presence of the sacred in flesh and blood." Anatheism is neither theism, nor atheism, nor an amalgamation of the two in the form of a grand subsumption: "Anatheism does not propose a new God, a new belief, a new religion. It simply invites us to see what has always been there *a second time around—ana.*"[23]

Our world has never needed us to begin again as it does now. With rampant militarism, unparalleled environmental degradation, mass incarceration decidedly biased against African Americans and Latin@s, and mounting tensions between people groups we need a do-over. As darkness is seeming to choke out more and more of the light inaugurated in Jesus Christ, we must lean into the power/possibility—the Greek word *dunamis* can mean both power and possibility—of becoming children of God (John 1:5).

Radical theologies of scripture do not grant us this power/possibility in and of themselves; rather, they deliver us from ourselves, our Western rationality and ways of being in the world. Radical theologies of scripture structure counterintuitive paths that move backwards in order to move forwards; they dig to the roots of the trees in order to find purchase above them. Radical theologies of scripture structure a kind of negative path—a *via negativa*—that participates in the life-affirming, liberative way with God in the World. They are the impossibility of impossibility, which doesn't quite add up to a possibility, but exposes us to the God for whom all things are possible.

Part III

This Is How We Do It:
Reading the Bible Today

God can give himself to be thought without idolatry only start-
ing from himself alone:
to give himself to be thought as love, hence as gift; to give him-
self to be thought as a thought of the gift.
— JEAN-LUC MARION[1]

Modern Christianity sucks. Oftentimes I open my Internet browser to read the headlines and I have to double-check to make sure that I didn't accidently stumble onto an episode of *True Blood*. #Godhatesfangs Christians the world over kill, lie, steal, rape the earth, abuse women, hate Muslims, bomb clinics, protest marriage equality, watch Fox News, and commit any number of other atrocious acts—all too often in the name of Jesus. It's bedlam out there.

Too many self-proclaimed Jesus-followers are actually Jesus-proclaimed self-followers. Jesus said, "If y'all wanna be my friends, you gotta love people. You gotta deny your selfish impulses and serve others, dammit!" (Luke 9:23). As part of a community of so-called disciples, I shudder at our attempts to follow Jesus' teachings. It makes me want to toss my Precious Moments Bible in the recycling bin—at least by recycling it I would be doing something positive for the world.

So, what are we to do? Do we hop aboard the spiritual-not-religious train? I, for one, refuse to go quietly into that good night. With all the raginess we can muster, I believe that we must drive a stake through the heart of modern Christianity in order to save the church.

Christians cannot hate the world with their words and deeds and claim Christ in their hearts. If you hate people it's just as bad as killing them (Matt. 5:21). We are supposed to be vessels of God's love. We ought to be the first to respond to injustice, environmental degradation, abuse, and hunger. Instead we behave like teenagers being drug out of bed on a Saturday morning to chop wood in the snow. We are supposed to be salt and light.

Inside our churches things are no better. Sometimes when I'm in a church I get the feeling like I'm in a scene from *Fight Club*: dilapidated church buildings, burnt Maxwell House coffee, people pounding one another bloody at church business meetings—at least the corpulent deacons wear shirts. Are we the beloved community, or, to quote Tyler Durden, are we the "all-singing, all-dancing crap of the world"? And Jesus said, the world would know we are his followers by how we love one another (John 13:35). Lord, have mercy!

There are exceptions to all of this, of course. There are moments of beauty that break through the clouds of my cynicism. Some Christ-followers remind me that there's still hope for the church. But as a whole we fall woefully short of embodying a Jesus kind of love—myself included. If Jesus really lives in our hearts, ought not such love be visible? Unless we move toward a new way of living, a way that looks kinda, maybe, sorta like Jesus, the church will die and so it should.

God calls us to a different way of speaking, living, and behaving in the world. We are called to love our neighbors and to love our God. But this is not multiple choice; it's not an either/or. Loving God entails loving your neighbor. Loving your neighbor shows the world that you love God.

I believe that it's so damn difficult to lean into a Jesus kind of life today because Western ways of relating to God and others have so thoroughly saturated our hearts and minds that we can't make love happen. *Love is antithetical to the modern mindset.* Descartes screwed us all.

Think about it. We don't destroy the earth because we are horrible, evil bastards. We destroy the earth because we care more about the bling-bling than we do about the impact our capitalist greed will have on future generations. We don't tolerate the presence of unjust lending practices, for-profit prisons, food deserts, or inadequate healthcare because we want to watch other people suffer. Not most of us, anyway—certainly not you; you wouldn't still be reading this book, otherwise. We allow these things to continue because it's too easy to turn other people into objects, mere things that can be discarded or ignored. But the church can do better. We must foster ways to recognize that everyone is created in God's image and is worthy of love, respect, and care. #wecandoit #aintgonnabeeasy

Throughout this book I've been building toward an alternative path to understanding scripture and through scripture the world: the path of love. But for love to really make a difference in our lives we must allow it to transform our *minds* (Rom. 12:2) and our *attitudes* (Phil. 2:5). We need a different approach—an erotic approach—that enables us to think and feel on a different register than the one promulgated by modern Christianity today.

Making love with scripture opens just such an alternative path toward God's Word revealed in scripture, and at the same time it opens a relationship between us and others. It enables us to regard all of creation, and especially people, as beloved by God and worthy of love. Because God so loved the world, we are free to regard our neighbors with the same degree of love and compassion that we have for ourselves.

The mental transformation that is required by the erotic approach begins by moving away from seeking *what* biblical texts mean, to discerning *how* they mean. Indeed, unless we attend to how biblical texts mean we are incapable of discerning what they mean for contemporary faith and practice—it's like trying to understand Groot apart from Rocket's translations. #Iamgroot

Making love with scripture calls us to put a bullet between the eyes of our ideological, theological, and biblical assumptions, straight-up gangsta style. *sings, "16 in the clip and one in the hole"; grabs daughter's supersoaker* *click. click.* The erotic approach that supports and guides an erotic theology of scripture employs an erotic logic—a love that overwhelms logic—as its guiding light. In short, love offers the means by which our minds are renewed and reoriented to God and neighbor.

Having tasted the fruits of liberation and radical theologies of scripture—forbidden fruits for some—we are now in a position to harvest them, to distill a new varietal suitable to our current cultural contexts and sufficient to the challenges we face in our globalized, fractured, and environmentally fragile world. *opens box of muscadine wine. fills red Solo cup* What? Don't be a snob. It's what my people drink when we write theology. *slurp, slurp*

In spite of all they teach us, liberation and radical theologies are not enough because critique is not an end in itself. We must not rest at the point of negation. Nay-saying must open up a new yea-saying or we will slip into nihilism. What we need is a negation of negation, a life-affirming biblical *hell-yeah* that refuses to fall victim to the very resentment earlier theologies resolved to combat.[2] Of course, this doesn't mean that we have to relish everything we put in our mouths (I'm looking at you, Guy Fieri). But we do need a *positive* way forward that harbors and preserves a living memory of the *negative* way.

We need an *erotic* theology of scripture, one that opens us to a way of knowing God and neighbor *in love*, which is the only way to truly know either. Making love with scripture leads us beyond the ways of knowing propagated by modernity, which teaches us to turn God and neighbor into objects about which we can be certain and thereby control.

Modernity teaches us to break two of God's most important commandments: *Worship God alone* and *Don't kill anybody* (Exod. 20:4, 13). We've already looked at how Jesus reframes these commandments more positively, calling us to love God and neighbor with all that we are. How do we break these commandments? Well, for starters, when we treat the Bible as if it's more than a *witness* to God, we allow it to supplant God's supremacy. Scripture is not God. Likewise, when we siphon the life out of other people by reducing them to mere *things* that can be ignored, we are guilty of murder. When I can reduce a person to an *ist* (e.g., heterosexist, colonist, fundamentalist, capitalist, Willie Nelsonist), I can justify my hatred of them and my refusal of fellowship. When I can discount protestors as "hooligans" or "thugs," I convince myself that I can ignore their pain and their righteous indignation.[3]

The whole rest of this book is about how to read the Bible in love. How to make love *with* the Bible. Because, honestly, that's the only right way to read it, and to use it.

What Is Love? Baby, Don't Hurt Me

Love is difficult to define.[4] Like the last moments of a dream, or explanations as to why Lady Gaga is famous, the more we talk about love the less plausible we sound. This challenge is exacerbated by the fact that much that masquerades as love in our society is not love, regardless of what Nicholas Sparks writes.

Following from scripture, I define love as a mode of engaging others that recognizes, rejoices, and responds to other people *as people*. Love refuses to kill. It doesn't turn people into things. Love lets a person be who she is before God: a beloved child of God. Love doesn't give a damn about Descartes's quest for certainty or selfhood because love wants the other person to be who he is. Love doesn't try to make the other change or conform. Love affirms the *oddness* of others. As the late, great pastor and youth leader Mike Yaconelli once put it: "Oddness is important because the most dangerous word in Western culture is *sameness*."[5] Love is odd.

There are (at least) four marks of love: 1) Love preserves life, it does not dissect or dismember; 2) Love leads to genuine knowledge of others and is unperturbed if such knowledge remains ambiguous and uncertain; 3) Love radically disrupts and destabilizes the knower/lover; and 4) Love *begins* with a genuine encounter with the other, it does not end there.

There are also several common misperceptions about love that we need to clear up.

First, love will never degrade a person to the status of a mere object. Pornography, for instance, is the antithesis of love because it turns a person into an object of mere desire. Love will never turn a person into a *thing*. Above all, love preserves the sanctity of another person.[6]

Second, in love there can be no distinction between *bodily* love and *spiritual* love, the most infectious disease of the Western Christian mind. By way of example, look at Augustine and Bernard of Clairvaux, each of whom the church has canonized. Augustine pits bodily love against spiritual love. Bernard, while less dualistic than Augustine, still creates a hierarchy between bodily love and divine love. And even though he doesn't share Augustine's contempt for the body, the goal for Bernard is to move us beyond bodily love to spiritual love of God for God's own sake.[7]

Third, love is singular, even if its manifestations are plural. In other words, if I love you, I love you. That's it. I rejoice in your uniqueness and respect your otherness completely. Problems arise when we start to parse love into different categories (e.g., brotherly/sisterly love, sexual love, unconditional love). A lot of Christians do this—you may have heard talks on the different forms of love in the Bible from your youth pastor. I'm telling you, they're wrong.

This does not mean that love ought to manifest itself in the same way for everyone you love, merely that love is love regardless of how it is enacted between the one person and another. Love is love, or it is nothing. It's not uncommon to hear Christ-followers, especially nerdy Christ-followers (like me) who study Greek in seminary or college, to make a big-ass deal over the different words the Bible uses for love (e.g., *phileo, eros, agape*). To the contrary, this argument cannot be substantiated intellectually or semantically (the verb *agapan*, for instance, is used in the Septuagint [the Greek translation of the Old Testament] to describe Amnon's illicit and abhorrent love for Tamar [2 Samuel 13:1-4] and in the New Testament for Demas's love for the world [2 Timothy 4:10]).[8]

The final point of clarification I wish to make is between *love* and *logic*. These words are often viewed as antonyms. They are folded into the same dualistic opposition that divides rationality, sameness, presence, and being from their imagined opposites: madness, otherness, absence, and nothingness.

Love is not otherwise than the intellectual, the rational, or the possible. Rather, it rejects the boundary between the intellectual and the emotional, the rational and the irrational, possibility and impossibility. Paradoxically, Paul prays that the Ephesians will come *"to know* the love of Christ that *surpasses knowledge"* (3:19). Knowledge that surpasses knowledge is still knowledge, but on a higher register. Love pees in the pool of Western modernity. (Ignore that warm spot. Keep swimming, people. Nothing happening here.) Love abides by its own logic. It swells up within logic and bursts it open.

At base, love refuses to harm other people—*baby don't hurt me, no more.* As the Apostle Paul explains in 1 Corinthians 13, love is not selfish. It doesn't use people for its own ends. As such, it protects the uniqueness of the other and rejoices in the oddness that makes the other who he is. It approaches the other barefooted, because the space love opens up between the self and the other is holy ground. Even as love is driven by a desire to be in relation with the other, it is halted by care for the other—so maybe love doesn't pee in the pool, but not because it can't; but for the other's sake, because it doesn't want the other to swim in pee water. Thanks, love!

The question that arises out of these reflections on love is what this has to do with theologies of scripture and biblical meaning-making. The answer is simple: love opens the only way to receive God's Word in the world beyond collapsing God into an ideology or turning a person into an object. Now, let me show you how.

Chapter Eight

Selflessness and Bravery
Aren't All That Different:
The Self before the Wor(l)d

[Jesus] presents a new intensity of covenantal love greater than the power of death, love that leads to new life. This new must be chosen. It requires social death for the sake of new life.
— WILLIE JENNINGS[1]

People can be such jerks. Modernity makes our jerkiness come all the more easily. Since our goal is to learn how better to love God and neighbor in and through scripture, we gotta start with good ole numero uno: us. Love is not gonna emerge miraculously out of the Bible just because you ask nicely. It ain't like popping a zit. Love requires a serious gut-check. Since modernity placed the solitary thinking being at the center of life, this is where we must start.

How we get this whole erotic thing up in the air, however, might just surprise you.

By way of example, meet Tris. She's a sixteen-year-old girl born into a post-apocalyptic society marked by difference—literally. You see, Tris's world is stratified according to personality types. Some are brave. Some are kind. Others are selfless. In Tris's world, people are segregated according to their aptitudes and personalities into one of five factions: Abnegation, Candor, Amity, Erudite, or Dauntless. In case you didn't know, this is the world of *Divergent*, a young adult dystopian novel written by Veronica Roth.

In the world of *Divergent*, children are forced to join one of these five factions when they turn sixteen. The faction they join may or may not be the faction in which they were brought up. Born into the Abnegation faction, Tris was reared in austere conditions: plain food, plain clothes, simple acts of selflessness. But Tris never felt quite right in Abnegation; she perceived herself as not selfless enough, and so, when her moment of decision arrived, she chose to join Dauntless.

Bravery is the number one virtue of the Dauntless faction. In spite of the radical differences from her home faction, Tris thrives in her new environment. Fast forward through the base jumping, zip-lining off 100 story buildings, tattooing, knife throwing, street fighting, and *really* awkward teenage love scenes, and we arrive at a moment of revelation for Tris.

At this point in the novel she's speaking with Tobias, her Dauntless instructor and soon-to-be man candy. Tris has been feeling like she doesn't quite belong in Dauntless, that she doesn't belong anywhere because she is, duh, divergent. In other words, she doesn't fit into any *one* faction, but manifests traits of multiple factions. Oh to be a misunderstood, self-obsessed teenager again. *dons old letter jacket; plays Alanis Morissette CD; flips through yearbook*

As Tris's feelings of alienation and dissonance from her society and even herself reach their climax, Tobias offers an insight that becomes what I take to be the thesis of the novel, indeed the whole trilogy. Tobias declares, "Selflessness and bravery aren't all that different."

Tobias is right, and his insight transcends the dystopian world Roth depicts, bleeding into our own dystopian world marked with its own racial and economic stratifications, political and religious exclusiveness, and xenophobia—even by our own justice system, which is supposed to be blind to difference.

Selflessness and bravery are inextricable. Both call upon certain qualities in the self, qualities that are interrelated and mutually dependent.

It takes bravery to be selfless, to humble yourself, to minimize your ego, to risk your self on behalf of another. Likewise, selflessness is necessary for bravery. There is no bravery apart from some degree of risk to the self, without some skin in the game, as they say. Selflessness and bravery go together like weed and Wiz Khalifa—can't have one without the other. Okay, maybe you can have the former without the latter, but why would you want to?

Furthermore, you'll never find selflessness and bravery taking place in a vacuum. To be selfless I require others whom I may approach in humility and service; to be brave I must confront circumstances that elicit fear in me so that I may *choose* to act bravely.

At bottom, other people make us who we are. How we treat people shapes who we are in our innermost selves. Every foreground requires a background—not as its opposite, but as its condition of being. You cannot profess to be a progressive apart from the societal conditions out of which you are progressing. You can't see yourself as an environmentalist apart from an environment in peril. You can't claim to be a drunken hippo wrangler apart from, well, drunken hippos. We need others for us to be who we are.

And ultimately, selflessness and bravery are only possible by action. They are things that you *do*. You cannot be brave or selfless in your heart and mind and then do nothing to effect change in the world. Even Care Bears gotta get their Care Bear stare on. Take *that*, Skeletor!

Hey, God Loves You!

Spaghetti-stained T-shirt and all, God loves you. You can do nothing to change this. In Jeremiah 31:3 we learn that God loves us with "an everlasting love." Everlasting means . . . wait for it . . . that it lasts forever. No matter what you do. It's important that we recognize this. So take a minute and let it sink in, like in that scene from *Good Will Hunting* when Matt Damon experiences the truth that all the bad stuff in his past is not his fault. God loves you.

Whenever we love another, God has already loved us. Every lover is a belated lover. She is tardy to the party, so to speak, because God has already loved her. She is already claimed as a beloved. This is the source of her limitless power and the *true* source of her identity. Society cannot define who she is. Nobody is Asian or differently abled or Republican without *first* being one who is loved by God. You can never, ever (and just so it sinks in) *ever* escape God's love.

Many of us already know what love feels like. Before we know how to talk, or walk, or use the big-boy potty, or twerk, most people already know what it feels like to be loved. Parents are usual suspects for such love. Teachers, siblings, pastors, that creepy mailman with the eyepatch who turns out to be a really swell guy, can also lead us to knowledge of love. Most creatures are born into and borne by love. With exceptions that we must not ignore or lightly dismiss, children are born into love. Before we have any sense of self, we are already defined as one who is beloved. Rather than merely *thinking* that I am, *à la* Descartes, I am because I am beloved.[2]

God's Word, revealed in Holy Scripture, allows us to comprehend our status as beloved more fully. Jesus tells his friends, "Y'all ain't gonna find a better love than this: to lay down yur life for yur friends" (John 15:13). Um, hold on, that's *exactly* what Jesus did for his friends! We wouldn't know the breadth or depth of love had the Creator of the cosmos not loved us enough to die for us, so that we might experience abundant life. And we wouldn't know this apart from scripture.

Much of scripture bears witness to God's love for us. The covenant story revealed in the Bible shows us both God's love for God's creation and God's ongoing presence in the world. In scripture we learn that God is a God who hears the cries of the oppressed and responds with covenantal love (Exod. 3:7). We discover in scripture that God loves the world (John 3:16). In scripture we learn that through Christ God is reconciling Godself with all things, on earth and heaven (Col. 1:20). I could list a hundred other examples, but you get the point: God loves you.

Remember your status as beloved. It's a source of tremendous power. When you fully experience the incontrovertible fact that the Creator of the universe loves you, you are able to humble yourself before God and neighbor. At the same time, your status as one beloved by God, people, and even creation itself, grants you the power to act out of a sense of boldness that defies whatever labels society casts upon you. Before you were born God knew you and loved you (Jer. 1:5; 29:11). Because you are God's beloved, you can love others (1 John 4:19).

The Way of the Cross: Humility *and* Boldness

How we approach other people shapes what we might receive from them. Westerners, following Descartes, have been taught to regard ourselves as subjects and all else that we encounter in the world of our experience as objects. Intersubjectively, modernity keeps us locked in a state of perpetual egocentrism like that of a three-year-old. However, every person I will ever encounter, and of course God, is also a *subject* and thus radically beyond objectification.[3] This creates a problem for knowing and speaking about God, but the cross of Christ provides a solution.

Parental Advisory: be wary of simplistic explanations of what actually happened when Jesus was crucified. However we choose to interpret the theological significance of Christ's death—as an act of Divine retribution borne by Jesus on behalf of sinful humanity, or as the ultimate act of Divine participation in human alienation and forsakenness—we cannot deny that it was an act of love.

I want to suggest that the way of love revealed by Jesus on the cross is one of selflessness *and* bravery. It was an act of ultimate divestment *and* an act of radical boldness; as such, it is a model for we who would follow Christ today.

When reflecting upon the cross, most commentators are quick to note Christ's divestment—his utter abnegation of his glory and withholding of his power.[4] The way of the cross for we who would follow Jesus, we who would "take up our own crosses," as it were, is clearly a path of humility. By letting go of ourselves, by stripping ourselves bare existentially and spiritually for the sake of the other, by abandoning our very sense of self, the Christ-follower opens himself to the way of God in Jesus Christ.

The way of love is the way of selflessness.

To be *for* the other is to limit myself on the other's behalf. Selflessness and restraint of my freedom define love at a fundamental level. This is what the Apostle Paul celebrates in his much-lauded hymn in Philippians 2. God *emptied* Godself to enter into creation in the person of Jesus Christ. Furthermore, God incarnate further *humbled* himself to the point of death—even death on a cross!

God's way of being in the person of Jesus Christ is the supreme act of abnegation. And God's work in and through Jesus defines love for us—"God displays God's love for us in that while we were still alienated from God, Christ died for us" (Rom. 5:8). But if we stop our reflections at selflessness and humility we fail to see the whole picture being painted by Christ's death on the cross.

It's easy to be blown away by the awesome display of God's self-sacrificial love on Golgotha. It's easy to think that following

Christ is to act humbly, to deny self. Such a theology is 100 percent true. At the same time, if this is all we have to say about Jesus' crucifixion and our continued participation in his death as his followers, then it is *also* 100 percent false.

Christian theology professes that Jesus was totally God *and* totally human. He was not half-god and half-human; he was not a demigod like Perseus or Hercules or Chris Hemsworth. So, when we look to the cross of Christ and hop on the humility train, we neglect that the Jesus being crucified was also *completely* human. He was just like you and me.

Theologies that see only God's divestment in Jesus' crucifixion flatten the cross to a single dimension.

The cross teaches us humility to be sure, but it also teaches us boldness. It shows us what genuine bravery looks like, which is the obverse side of love.

In his humanity, Jesus was born under imperial occupation. He was a subject of Roman rule. Jesus had no political power before the state. He was utterly subjugated by imperial decree. Furthermore, in his humanness Jesus was on the margins of his own society in terms of both the religious establishment and economic systems of his day.[5] His followers may have called him "Rabbi," but he was not vetted for the job. Jesus was a Rabbi to the same degree that Rick Ross is a boss or George Strait is a king. To put this in modern Christian terms, Jesus was guilty of preaching without a license. He was not ordained, that is, he was not vetted by the "approved" human institutions.

All this is to say that Jesus knew what it felt like to be on the margins of his society. A bastard in the eyes of humanity, his movement out of the cultural shadow in which we was born into the light of religious, cultural, and political life was an act of radical boldness—seriously, when you look up "boldness" in the dictionary you ought to find two entries: Jesus marching on Jerusalem and Tom Selleck's chest hair.

That Jesus would muster the temerity to challenge the religious, political, and economic structures of his day from this position of marginality must not be overlooked.

Jesus did not approach his cross by accident. In Luke's Gospel we read that as Jesus sensed that the time of his ascension was drawing near, he "set his face firmly toward Jerusalem" (9:51). Jesus displayed resolve. We see this again as Jesus prays in Gethsemane (Matt. 26:36-46). To participate in the way of Jesus is to follow him from the margins toward the seats of power, to speak truth to power, to fight to set the captives free.

Inasmuch as we take Jesus' humanity seriously, we will advocate nothing but boldness for those on the margins of our own society, those who have been denied agency. Theologian Tony Jones is right: "The way of the cross demands nothing less than total commitment to solidarity with others, especially those who are lonely and outcast." Jones follows this up by saying that "if Jesus' death does not provoke that kind of love in us, then we're not truly understanding the magnitude of the cross."[6]

The Erotic Approach, Step One: Loving Yourself

The way of Jesus on the cross—the way of humility and boldness—shows us how to approach God and neighbor in and through scripture. The erotic approach begins by moving toward God and neighbor with a Jesus-sized love. It requires from us deep humility to deflate our egos so that we don't reduce everyone we meet to a thing to be known with certainty, *and* it demands a radical boldness to be ready to fight for abundant life and human flourishing.

If you want to know God you must first love God. If you want to know someone as neighbor you must find a way to love her. And of course love of God and neighbor are not mutually exclusive.[7] The only way that you can love anyone (or anything) is by first deciding to situate yourself in such a way that the one you choose to love is free to exist in and for himself. At the same time, you can only love if you are a subject, an agent capable of acting on the world. This is not easy or simple. Loving is both radically passive and radically active.

Especially in our Western contexts, marked as they are by the will-to-power and control of people, bracketing yourself will require tremendous effort. It's a bit like the act of apparating in the *Harry Potter* series, where a witch or wizard teleports almost instantaneously from one location to another. By this the mind and body seem to come undone. Just try not to splinch yourself. #acciodittany

Paradoxically, by the erotic approach, the first step forward is also a step backward.[8] The advance is a retreat. Boldness and humility, even if different from person to person, are opposite sides of the same coin. Trying to separate them is as impossible as trying to take a pair of scissors and cut one side of paper without at the same time cutting the other.[9]

We witness this so clearly with Jesus in the Gospels. His bold advance against imperial and religious oppression is *also* a letting go of his claim to (Divine) selfhood. The first step to making love with scripture is made by this double movement of boldness and humility. Making love *with* scripture means that we advance *through* scripture by following scripture's gaze to the creatures whom God *also* loves. The first step to making love with scripture unravels the self (in a Western sense) even as it unfurls the self toward other creatures—both human and non. The self who loves loves first for the sake of loving.[10]

Example: Playing Host

I warned you that the erotic approach would be a bumpy ride. We are working against 500 years of conditioning, mind, so it's only to be expected that transforming how we understand ourselves will stretch our thinking in new ways. I think that some of the confusion may be cleared up with a concrete example. The function of the host and/or hostess is something we're all familiar with, and it can lead us to just what I'm getting at with this first step of the erotic approach.[11]

In Western thought, to be a self is to be a subject. Much as the protagonist of a story is free to effect change, to act upon her storied world, to be the main character in her story, the self is the agent of her own life—unless George R. R. Martin is writing the story, and then the protagonist is always already under a death sentence. *moves index finger slowly across throat*

From liberation theologians we have learned, however, that not every self has been granted equal access to selfhood. Ethnic, gender, and sexual minorities, as well as the environment, have all been denied selfhood to varying degrees. How can we love with a Jesus kind of love if the structures of inequity and injustice at work in our world deny us the agency to love ourselves, denying our very selfhood?

Imagine I just invited you to a party at my house. What do I do? Well, I vacuum the rug. I stock up on some adult beverages. I purchase the new Barry Manilow album on iTunes. I slip into that houndstooth smoking jacket with the corduroy elbow patches that makes me feel just a little bit naughty, but not too much to make my guests uncomfortable.

What happens when folks arrive? They ring the doorbell and I greet them warmly into my home. Right? Oh, I'm sorry, were you distracted by my houndstooth smoking jacket and my Manilow dance moves? Yeah, you know you were.

We all know what it feels like to play host, but have you ever thought about how the very act of *playing host* is both active and passive? This is true even at a semantic level.

The word *host* is rich. It diverges in English from its Latin root to mean in two very different ways. The one is linked with *hospitality* and the other is linked with notions of *hostility,* both of which remain alive within the term *host.* The internal tension always in play within the concept of playing host cannot be dismissed or overlooked.

Playing host, strictly speaking, is impossible. To *show* hospitality—to play host to another person—I must first be *master* to some extent. Think about it. How can I invite you into a house that is not mine? When I play host I am simultaneously displaying my power and displaying my restraint. I create a space for you in a place that remains my own. As my guest, I allow you to share in my hospitality, to "make yourself at home" without my home ever becoming *your* home.

Furthermore, to maintain hospitality, to remain your host, I must remain in power over you to some extent. If a robber breaks into my home, I am not his host. He has seized that possibility from me; it's the first thing that he steals from me. He cannot be my guest because he has already asserted himself according to a different relation: as an intruder.

This internal tension is why hospitality is simultaneously possible and impossible. Genuine hospitality demands a certain nonmastery, a certain abnegation of all claims to property, power, or ownership. At the same time, hospitality requires a certain level of control, forcing me to place limits on my guests.

In playing host, I also assert myself before you. Even as I invite you to make yourself at home in a home that is always mine, there is an invisible line that I will not permit you to cross. You can't cook my rhododendron or thrash my dog or chew on my coffee table. At these and an infinite number of other points, the hostility that remained dormant within my hospitality will come to life. This is true for even the most hospitable of hosts. Mr. Rogers himself would totally lose his shit if you screwed with his train set or hid one of his slippers—okay, maybe not, but it's certainly interesting to imagine. #wontyoubemyneighbor

Making love with scripture proceeds according to this ambiguous, tenuous sense expressed by playing host. The erotic approach to God and neighbor in and through scripture opens by the double movement of humility and boldness. It is an existential and spiritual attitude where I simultaneously will to love you as you are, to create a space for you in my place, to regard you as a *subject* beloved by God. Accordingly, in stepping back in on my selfhood I am also committing to step forward in defense of your selfhood, to assert myself boldly and bodily where I find you rooted in a particular culture and way of life.

The space of love participates in the ambiguities and richness of playing host because both take shape according to a kind of clearing of space within the self (humility) and *at the same time*, by asserting the self not as knower but as lover (boldness) it draws a line, a mark of hostility, at the threshold of encounter beyond which the other may not cross.

Embracing a Bold Humility

The way of God in Jesus Christ calls for a bold humility. This is true across socio-economic strata and geo-political divides. What situates us in our cultural particularities is how such a bold humility will be made manifest in the world.

If you're a mostly straight, white, educated, man such as myself, then you are required to do everything in your considerable power to advocate for those who do not share your societal privileges. The more power you've received, the more bold humility you ought to exercise. That's what Jesus did, ya know, God incarnate! However, it is crucial to note that even as you choose to follow in the way of Jesus in defense of the marginalized and oppressed, this doesn't make you Jesus. Solidarity is what we are after, not a hoard of dancing baby messiahs.

Most people of the world cannot check all of the privilege boxes. For such folks, their social identity is more complicated. They simultaneously benefit from and are marginalized by systems of power. Where oppression and marginalization are felt most palpably, that's where such people ought to exercise their boldness for themselves and others who share their plight. Don't let anyone make you feel like you are anything less than one beloved of God.

At the same time, where minoritized persons enjoy the benefits of power and privilege—and if you can read this book, at least you have the power of education, putting you in a privileged position over 800 million people—they are called through scripture to exhibit a Jesus-sized boldness in service of God and neighbor.

So, the first step of the erotic approach is that of loving yourself beyond the confines of Western modernity. We love, therefore we are. We are because we are beloved. Love unravels our selfhood in the modern sense, and it is in such an unraveling that we're opened to the other—God, human, and non-human—in love. This step may not appear to be a very big one, maybe just a baby step, but if all who have been summoned to love God in the way of Jesus would take this tiny shuffle in ourselves, there's no way of imagining what a difference we could make.

Chapter Nine

What Does the Fox Say?
Listening to the Wor(l)d

*So a theology of becoming begins more or less here, at the edges
  of a long silence.
A silence vibrant with the unspoken Word.*
                                              — CATHERINE KELLER[1]

The top trending song of 2013, played incessantly by tweens and
teens until the ears of American parents bled, was "The Fox." The
song was written and performed by the Norwegian comedy duo
Ylvis as a spoof intended to drive traffic to Ylvis's talk show. What
was meant to be an anti-hit turned out to be a breakout song for
Ylvis, soaring to #6 on the *Billboard* Hot 100.

The song, along with its accompanying music video, totters
between the surreal and the sublime. The premise of the song is
quite clever: What *does* the fox say? We all know that dogs go *bark*,
cats go *meow*, and cows go *moo*; but how many people have actually
experienced the vocal capacity of this mischievous mammal?

Foxes are not known to be particularly loquacious. The fox's call, like its overall personality, is mysterious. That's part of its allure. I believe that the song's virality transcends its catchy electronica beats, absurd lyrics, and handsome Scandinavian men frolicking through the forest in animal costumes. The song asks a question that many of us have never considered—what does the fox say?—and once the query is posed, it gives rise to thought.

In many ways, Holy Scripture is like the surreptitious fox. As soon as we encounter it, it holds our gaze in such a way that we cannot turn away. And yet, as we gaze transfixed upon it, it says nothing, content to patter silently into the woods. As with the fox, when we engage scripture we listen. Sight gives way to sound, but the Word offers no sound except for those "with ears to hear." It is a sound discernible only according to the ears of faith, which knows nothing with certainty. "That is why we have to read sacred Scriptures as carefully as we greet strangers in the night."[2]

Listening *to* the Word manifested in and through scripture is predicated on a listening *for* the Word. Such a listening is not a simple listening, a simple hearing. It is a listening foreshadowed by Elijah in the desert where God's Word comes as a "gentle whisper" (1 Kgs. 9:12). Or, as a more contemporary writer puts it, "The presence of the all-powerful Word in the book that is the Bible is a humbled presence, and it is as if a perpetual descent of God toward us."[3] Such a humbled presence requires a certain listening. It is according to such a listening that we open the conditions for the possibility of receiving God's Wor(l)d—an impossibility that is made possible to us by God alone.

The Wor(l)d of God

When we say that we listen for the Wor(l)d of God revealed in and through scripture, what exactly are we talking about? Well, a better question might be, *where* are we talking about?

Does God reveal Godself through scripture or creation? This question, which has played on repeat on the mixed-tape of power ballads that is Christian theology, is about as ludicrous as asking if Chris Rock is funnier as an actor or comedian. The answer, of course, is "Yes."[4]

God reveals Godself through scripture *and* creation. I could proof-text the hell out of this from scripture itself, but I won't—well, okay, just one, because you asked, you saucy minx, you: "Where can I flee from your presence? If I climb up to heaven, you are there; if I descend into Sheol, you are there also" (Ps. 139:7-8).[5] Inasmuch as God exists within the bounds of our notions of space and time, God "is" everywhere.

There is no part of scripture that is not utterly *in* the world, and yet, the world cannot contain or comprehend all that is made known to us about God in and through scripture. As a sunken ship contains part of the sea and is entirely contained by the sea, scripture is entirely in the world without the world being entirely in scripture. That's what my mash-up word "Wor(l)d" signifies.

Just as it is crazy to think of individuality apart from community, to think of church apart from society, to think of Hootie apart from the Blowfish, we cannot think of God apart from the world. This doesn't mean, however, that the one is equal to the other. God is not (only) the world. God isn't reducible to life. But neither is God reducible to what the Bible says about God.

The Wor(l)d of God is a paradox. God's self-revelation is *also* God's self-concealment. God presents Godself to us as the "divine incognito."[6] Our finite human minds cannot grasp God's Wor(l)d, but it is precisely this grasping, this yearning, that God has elected to honor.

When we invoke the name "God," that which we name is radically beyond the name itself and all possible names (Eph. 1:21). The name "God" at once participates in the name, condescending to the limits of our language and intellect, and at the same time withdraws from the name. The name "God" is a sign of the incompleteness of all discourse on God.

It is precisely on account of God's otherness, revealed to us as and according to God's Wor(l)d, that we must listen with the ears of love. But the one thing that cannot be ignored or reduced when we think about listening is the notion of distance. If you are too far away from me I won't hear a word you say. If you are too close, with your lips on my ears, say, I won't be able to process the vibrations of your voice into meaningful sound in my ears. Try it sometime; it's a blast at parties.

As with listening, distance is crucial for love. We've already seen that the way of love does not objectify the other. In other words, love refuses to close the gap between you and me. The moment we stop seeking, yearning, listening *in love* for God's Wor(l)d revealed in and through scripture, we are guilty of idolatry.

All this is to affirm in a new way the confession of the church that Jesus Christ is the Word of God, fully present and completely transcendent at the same time. Christ is both midnight and midday. And even as Jesus is the fullest expression of God's Word, the World of God that he inaugurates is a vacuum that draws all of creation into the miracle of God.[7] The words of the biblical text and the world in which we live bear witness to God's radical otherness: the Wor(l)d.

Loving the Other: A Deconstructive Parable of Liberation

In Luke 10:25-37 Jesus tells a parable to an expert in the Judaic law, offering us the deepest understanding of how we are to make love with scripture: by turning our vision and actions toward the other in need.

Jesus opens us to a certain vision and a certain way of approaching other people that subverts our propensity to treat them as mere objects. A lawyer—not like a Judge Judy lawyer, but a religious expert (read: Bible scholar)—asks Jesus what he must do to achieve a long life (I don't know why, but I always picture this dude speaking with a French accent).

Rather than responding directly, Jesus tosses the question back at him, asking, "What has been written in the law and how have you interpreted it?"

Let's pause here to underline something that Jesus notes, as it's something I've been stressing all along: there is a difference between *what* is written and *how* it is read or interpreted. Jesus' twofold query highlights the tension between the two poles of text and interpretation. This tension is not an obstacle to be overcome to discern biblical meaning, but is necessary for the very possibility of meaning and even truth.

The Bible scholar responds by quoting two passages from the Hebrew Scriptures (i.e., what has been written). Big shocker! He asserts that the key to a long life is to love God with all of one's heart, mind, soul, and strength and to love one's neighbor as oneself. Boo-yah! Take that, Jesus! *man drops mic. exits stage* By the way, the two parts of the Bible scholar's recipe for long life are from Deuteronomy 6 and Leviticus 19, respectively. Remember this last bit. It'll come up later.

Jesus doesn't flinch. You see, The Reverend Dr. Smarty McSmartybritches only responded to half of Jesus' query; he quotes scripture verbatim, but the Bible scholar does not explicate or interpret its meaning. Nevertheless, Jesus tells the man that he has answered correctly and that if he does these things, he will live. Note that Jesus changes the Bible scholar's words. The man came to Jesus inquiring about "long life," but Jesus says only that if the man does these things he "will live." There is a difference between a long, full life—an abundant life—and merely living. For reals! (See Facebook.)

Luke then tells us that the Bible scholar—"wanting to justify himself"—asks a follow-up question: "So, ooh eez my neighbor?"

Again, rather than answering the question straight away, Jesus presents the Bible scholar with another question, this time in the form of a parable—a lil' narrative razzle-dazzle fo ya.

The tale Jesus tells is straightforward. A traveler is robbed, beaten, and left to die on the side of the road. Three sojourners see the man—a priest, a Levite, and a Samaritan—but only the Samaritan is selfless and bold enough to approach the injured stranger.

Jesus is careful with his stage direction here. Both the priest and the Levite, the religious leaders (read: pastor and seminary professor), "passed by on the other side" of the injured man, while the Samaritan "came to where he was" and "was moved with loving concern." The compassionate Samaritan man tends to the stranger's wounds, sets him on his own donkey, and provides for the injured man extravagantly out of his own resources.[8] Note the progression. He recognizes the other, is moved with concern for the other, and responds materially to the needs of the other at great personal cost.

Jesus then flips the question back to the Bible scholar. "So," Jesus asks, lighting a cigarette and taking a long, slow drag, "which of these three was a neighbor to the man who fell into the hands of robbers?" *Bearded Jesus exhales smoke*

Knowing he's lost the battle of wits, the Bible scholar responds, "Zee von who showed im zee covenantal love." Jesus nods and tells the man to go and do likewise.

This parable of the just neighbor offers us a framework for approaching others in and through scripture, and I believe this applies not only to human others.[9] Jesus shows us right here what making love with scripture really looks like: loving the other unconditionally.

The Erotic Approach, Step 2: Loving Your Neighbor

In the first step toward making love with scripture, I move toward you in humility and boldness, resolving not to reduce you to a mere object of my experience. Right? The second step of the erotic approach is opened up by the first. In the second step, I wait and I listen for you to present yourself to me in some way. This in no way binds you to show me anything. That's the risk I take in deciding to love. However, should you at this point choose to accept the offering of this space that I have given to you in love, then we have here forged a connection where genuine respect, care, and mutuality might emerge.

Jesus teaches us in his parable of the just neighbor that the other person to whom I draw near, to whom I make myself a neighbor, ought not be reduced to the designation *foreigner*. A foreigner is defined by her difference from the person in charge of the discourse—the subject, the "self" in a modern sense. What love does is flip the self-other relation upside down (umop apisdn. Get it? Give this book a 180 and you'll get it. Whoa! Just blew your mind, didn't I?).

Jesus himself deconstructs our relation to others, teaching us that love of neighbor requires that we "draw near" to another person. Only by this movement (the first step) can we set the stage for an encounter with someone as neighbor (the second step).

Every person I encounter is quintessentially a neighbor, which only happens when I *draw near* to him beyond certainty. Jesus' kung fu is strong here. In the context of Leviticus 19, which, you will recall, the Bible scholar was quoting when he spoke of loving one's neighbor as oneself, the designation "neighbor" was employed as an ethnocentric term. In other words, a neighbor was synonymous with a fellow Jew. The entire verse in Leviticus reads, "You shall not hate in your heart anyone of *your kin*; you shall reprove *your neighbor*, or you will incur guilt yourself. You shall not take vengeance or bear a grudge against any of *your people*, but you shall love *your neighbor as yourself*: I am the Lord" (19:17-18).

Jesus deconstructs the Bible scholar's ethnocentrism by redefining the way we think about people. The neighbor is not the one who *is* near, but the one who *draws* near by showing loving kindness. The just neighbor is a Samaritan, the quintessential foreigner within

Jesus' first-century socio-religious context. Recall that the priest, the Levite, and the Samaritan man all see the man in need, but only the Samaritan man is "moved with compassion." Only he becomes a neighbor to the man in need. This is what it means to love the other.[10]

Accordingly, the second step of the erotic approach requires that we take a different tack in how we receive other people than the traditional ways of modernity. Our most common way of perceiving the other, especially from a male perspective, is through sight. The pervasive male gaze is pretty much the easiest path to treating another as an object.[11] Why do you think that pornography is a billion-dollar industry, the vast majority of which is consumed by men? That is why I want to suggest the action of listening over looking for two reasons, both of which arise out of my reflections on Jesus' parable of the just neighbor.

First, listening requires proximity. You can see much farther than you can hear. That means that you reserve the freedom to ignore the other person's call for you to act justly, to show mercy. You can choose to "pass by on the other side." You can avert your gaze from life much easier than you can block out the cries of those who struggle for life.

Second, listening can be easily differentiated from hearing. Hearing is a sense that most people possess. For we who are blessed with this sense, it happens without any effort on our part. Sight works the same way, but you can close your eyes, you have a degree of control over this sense. At the same time, seeing is seeing, while listening is not necessarily the same thing as hearing.[12] I can hear you, but that doesn't mean I am listening. Listening in this sense finds support in the Apostle Paul's words by which we are able to discern the groans of creation (Rom. 8:22).

Listening toward Life: An Example from X-Men

The way of love that moves toward the neighbor is contextually situated and oriented toward the neighbor's flourishing.[13] Said differently, love of the neighbor ought to be radically open to his lived experiences and social conditions, particularly the struggles he faces. But all of this risks getting lost in the murkiness of theory-land, where I myself have erected a summer home. Drop on by sometime; you're welcome! We find an example of the kind of listening I'm pressing us to embrace in the movie *X-Men: Days of Future Past*. Don't smirk. It's a good one. It showcases an openness to the other in and through scripture required in this second step of the erotic approach.

The film's plot is quite involved. In brief, Wolverine's consciousness is projected back in time to 1973, where he must find and enlist the support of Professor X and Magneto in order to thwart a chain of events that will eventually wipeout all of mutantkind—hey, it's a comic book movie, the more grandiose the plot the better. #marveluniverse Wolverine's quest is complicated when he finds that the thirty-year-old version of Professor X has taken to alcoholism and drug abuse in order to numb his own telepathic powers.

At the turning point in the film, when Wolverine challenges Professor X to use his telepathy, Professor X confesses the reason he has anesthetized himself to his own powers. In a scene that raises the bar on awesomeness for an already awesome franchise, the young Professor X journeys into Wolverine's 1973 mind, travels through it into the Wolverine of the future's body, and there Professor X has a conversation with himself. *chest bumps random dude at coffee shop*

Young Professor X tells his future self that he can't bear to listen to the minds of others anymore because their pain overwhelms him. Old Professor X assures his younger self that the pain of others will actually make him stronger, but only if he allows himself to feel their pain at its fullest. Old Professor X says, "It's the greatest gift we have: to bear their pain without breaking. And it comes from the most human part of us: hope." As expected, these wise words provide the spark to ignite the young Professor X into action, and the good guys win the day.

This is the kind of listening I'm talking about for the second step of the erotic approach. When we open ourselves fully to another's pain and suffering in love, it inverts the polarity of our engagement with the neighbor, so to speak. In other words, it transforms me as a passive recipient of external information into an active agent in solidarity with another. Such listening is not a mere hearing, but one that is bolstered by hope borne *for* the other. Such a hope is born out of a loving engagement with the Word of God revealed in scripture and it is henceforth made available for the neighbor whom we love in the World who is marked by such loving concern. Only when we love in this way through scripture are we able to (bear) witness (to) the World of God.

The reasons for such a listening are both theological and ethical. Listening in this way attends to the murmurs and silences that disrupt both theology and ethics. A hopeful listening is always attentive to the neighbor's particularity. After all, the Wor(l)d of God has revealed Godself most fully in the *particular* person of Jesus Christ, who embodied a *particular* kind of listening. Jesus listened for calls of pain and injustice from the margins of society (the mentally ill, the differently abled, the economically disenfranchised, etc.) and such a listening was driven toward human flourishing and marked by hope.

Listening toward life is a double listening. It is not a sequential listening, but a kind of listening that hears with both ears, discerning at once the pains inherent in the struggles of many for life and God's summons to be radically oriented to the neighbor's flourishing. This is what it means, at its most basic sense, to be a Christ-follower. This double listening is both theological and ethical, while exceeding both.

With the one ear we listen toward life in terms of the lived realities of others. Ignoring God's incarnation in Jesus of Nazareth, in its particular, embodied instantiation in time and space produces universalizing theologies that miss God's revealed concern for the details of life.[14] That's why we took the time in part 1 of this book to attend to liberation theologies of scripture and to contextually rooted ways of interpreting scripture.

With the other ear—again, not by another listening, but at the same time—one listens toward life by listening to God's life-giving and boundary-breaking Word in the world that places us in the path of others, that makes us neighbors to and for other people.[15] In other words, we do not listen merely to understand the plight of the oppressed and marginalized, we listen so that we can discern what God would have us do about it, here and now.

The kind of listening that love elicits demands our engagement with not only the neighbor, but also the societal conditions that thwart her flourishing, that bar her from experiencing the abundant life promised by God in and through scripture. That's why we took the time in part 2 of this book to learn about deconstruction and the radical theologies of scripture inspired by such an approach to the Wor(l)d. See, y'all, don't let my snarkiness fool you; there's a method to this madness.

The Wor(l)d of Silence

The Wor(l)d spoken in and through the Bible is a Wor(l)d of silence. We are invited into this silence when we are willing to listen, to participate in God's revealed silence in love. We strain our ears in hope, knowing in our hearts that God speaks to us beyond our capacity to listen. It is then that the Wor(l)d speaks to us.[16] The Wor(l)d spoken to us is a call to be for the other with the same kind of superabundant love displayed by the Samaritan sojourner in Jesus' parable.

God's speaking is a claiming—God's claiming of us as beloved sons and daughters. Only by listening to the Wor(l)d at work in and through the words of Holy Scripture do we come to see that our approach to God is belated. God has already approached us. Our love of God can never be quick enough. God has already loved us, even in our alienation from God, precisely in our alienation from God. And God has a heart for lost things (Luke 15).

Lastly, let us never forget that the gate of God-knowledge can only be opened from within. The erotic path toward the other sets forth conditions that increase the possibility that God will speak beyond every impossibility. God can and has spoken to humans in many ways. God revealed Godself to Moses in a burning bush. God revealed Godself to Elijah through a faint, blowing whisper. God revealed Godself to Balaam through a donkey. God is still speaking to us today. We must listen with the ears of love that offer hope toward abundant life. That is our charge and our privilege as Christ-followers.

Chapter Ten

You Can't Handle the Truth: The Saturated Wor(l)d

The erotic is the nurturer or nursemaid of all our deepest knowledge.

— AUDRE LORDE[1]

Nearly every movie has a line or two that somebody can quote. Such phrases capture the pith of the film; they seize our imagination. Every once in a while, a phrase is uttered in a movie that *everybody* can quote. Such lines as "Life is like a box of chocolates," "I'll be back," "I'm the king of the world," and "Toto, I've a feeling we're not in Kansas anymore" are iconic. Their recitation transports us to the first time we saw the film.

In the film *A Few Good Men*, Jack Nicholson's character utters one of the most often-quoted lines in cinematic history: "You can't handle the truth!" It still gives me goosebumps.

Nobody can deliver this line like Nicholson. Mostly it's his trademark eyebrows and gravelly voice; but even more than that, the line carries a significance that transcends the film itself. Unlike the other lines we remember months or years after we've seen a film, this sentence requires no context. It is self-sufficient. Anything worthy of the name *truth* cannot be handled. It is defined, in a certain sense, by its unhandlability—which isn't a word, but it should be. How much more appropriate are Nicholson's words in the face of the Wor(l)d of God?

Like the truth, you can't *handle* the Wor(l)d. It cannot be manipulated or managed. It is unwieldy. If there is a "truth" to be had in the Bible it is beyond our grasp. That doesn't mean that the Wor(l)d is not true. Jesus, the Wor(l)d incarnate, tells us that he is the way, the truth, and the life (John 14:6). But can we handle it?

Truth is not something we can possess. You can't carry it in your pocket like chapstick or a lightsaber. When scripture talks about truth it does so in terms of a way of being; it is not inert but alive in the thoughts and behaviors of men and women (e.g., Ps. 25:5; 43:3). Furthermore, truth is always spoken of as something external to us (e.g., Gal. 2:5; James 5:19).

As we move toward the third step in the erotic approach to God's Wor(l)d, we need to understand what we might actually receive from God in and through scripture—from our contextually situated readings toward abundant life. We must come to a deeper appreciation for what we receive as Wor(l)d, as truth, because our Western mode of thinking has distorted this.

The Wor(l)d of God given in and through scripture cannot be handled; it can only be lived. Such a living constitutes the *World* inaugurated by God's *Word*, which is itself inaugurated by God's ongoing revelation through scripture. The Wor(l)d is like lava. Once it hardens it is no longer the Wor(l)d, but becomes a witness to the Wor(l)d. This is why deconstruction is the Bible reader's friend; it saves us from the idolatry to which we are ever prone.[2]

But how do we speak of such a Wor(l)d if every saying loses its vivacity in its very enunciation? The best way I've found to talk about the gift of God's self-revelation as God's Word in the world is through the metaphor of saturation. Because we are human and we are finite, and thus we are limited temporally, spatially, and intellectually, we cannot *handle the truth*. It overwhelms our capacities of reception and our ability to assimilate information.

Hear me clearly now: saturation is a metaphor. The Wor(l)d of God is not actually saturation. Rather, saturation is what we experience when we encounter the Word as gift, in love—as a gift of love that fills the world as we experience it to bursting. Be just as wary of folks who claim to have the truth as those who claim that there is no truth. Both participate in the same logic, a logic antithetical to God's self-revelation in and through scripture.

The Saturated Wor(l)d of God

Making love with scripture allows us to receive the gift of God's Wor(l)d revealed in and through scripture. Recall that the Wor(l)d of God renders both a transformation in our hearts and minds (Word) and an alternative way of being, a becoming in our daily lives (World). Initiated by a certain movement of the self toward God and neighbor in love and sustained by a certain listening to the other's call out of and toward life, we create the conditions of possibility for receiving God's Wor(l)d.

Recall that with love there are no guarantees. This is not like one of those seven-steps-to-a-happy-marriage programs. Love is the best approach to the Wor(l)d because it participates in the Wor(l)d's unwieldiness. Love is wild. It cannot be tamed, nor does it aim to tame the other. Making love with scripture is a way of participating in the Wor(l)d's tempestuousness in the way that we set the tack on our sail in line with the wind.

How then do we understand this equation? The self-in-love + the other-received-in-love < love. The equation is not balanced, nor can it ever be. That which we receive as Wor(l)d exceeds our steps to the Wor(l)d. This shouldn't surprise you. Jesus himself taught us that we who approach the Wor(l)d of God receive thirty, sixty, or a hundred times what was sown (Matt. 13:18-23). When we love, we give up the very thing that could balance the equation. Love employs its own set of scales, its own metrics. On the contrary, the self-as-subject + the other-as-object ≠ erotic knowledge.[3] In other words, when we reduce either God's Word or the neighbor to an object, what we glean is not the kind of knowledge oriented to the transformation of the world, but merely a paltry knowledge that never really leaves the self.

Here's the deal: if you can understand God's Wor(l)d you have not encountered God as Wor(l)d. If you can say absolutely and unequivocally "this is what the Bible means" or "this is the only social program of which God would be proud," then you are guilty of idolatry. The Wor(l)d of God cannot be objectified. It overwhelms us. In this way, it's kind of like love.

When we encounter God's Wor(l)d in love we are redefined by the very Wor(l)d we do not seek to possess, to keep safe in the pocket of our minds. We are not knowers, we are lovers. Though this is nevertheless a certain kind of knowing. Loving God with all of our being (with our heart, soul, mind, and strength), wherein we love our neighbors as ourselves, opens a way to the Wor(l)d that saturates our capacity to understand, to handle the truth.

The saturated experience overwhelms and exceeds our capacities to receive objects of experience.[4] It is like a light that is so bright that it ceases to illuminate anything. It blinds us with its own superabundance. Or, to use another analogy, it's like a food that simultaneously satisfies and yet increases our hunger with every bite. It's like trying to drink water from a fire hose. Even as you drink, think of how much water exceeds your capacity for consumption. It's just too much, too fast. In such a way, the Wor(l)d of God is bedazzling. Exactly like Jesus himself, it is found in the world but it is not of the world. It disrupts and overwhelms human knowledge (John 1:10).

The site where we encounter the other in love is always saturated. The movement in which I receive the Wor(l)d revealed in and through scripture is a saturated moment. The New Testament speaks of this as *kairos* time, which, while still operative within time, disturbs and overwhelms ordinary *chronos* time (e.g., Mark 1:15; Rom. 5:6). This is the moment in time and space where I decide to regard another with hospitality or hostility, to treat her as neighbor or foreigner, to receive her as beloved or as object.

The saturated Wor(l)d received by and according to love only exists as long as we maintain our erotic connection. As soon as I reassert myself as subject, as soon as I stop playing host to you, as soon as I stop listening, as soon as I try to *handle* you, this is the moment when love has ceased. That which I can possess is not the Wor(l)d. At best, it is a witness to the Wor(l)d.

Manna from Heaven, Bread on Earth

To understand what emerges out of willing love toward another and receiving that which the other gives when we listen deeply to life, we need look no further than the Bible. The revealedness that results from the erotic approach is like the bread God provided for God's people Israel in the wilderness as they followed Moses out of Egypt.

In Exodus chapter 16 we find the Israelites two-and-a-half months out from God's miraculous initiative to liberate them from Egyptian slavery. You can imagine that food wasn't too easy to come by in the wilderness—that's kind of the nature of designating an area of land "the wilderness." Anywho, the people start to grumble to Moses that it would've been better if they had never left Egypt. At least they had McDonald's and KFC to eat.

Moses has a little facetime with the Lord and God promises to provide food for the Israelites to prove that it was God who led them out of captivity and it was God who cares for them still. God does as God promises, sending a strange flaky substance to cover the ground—the way the Bible describes it makes the manna from heaven sound like it could taste like fortune cookies. Mmm. Fortune cookies. Now I'm hungry.

In this chapter we discover (at least) four things about God that can help us think about God's self-revelation in and through scripture by the erotic approach.

First, we witness a quality of God that is repeated over and over again throughout scripture and is testified by God's enduring presence in and through the church: God is responsive to the cries of human suffering, and it is by God's responsiveness that God reveals Godself. We witness this clearly in verse 12, where the Lord explains to Moses that God has heard the cries of the people and God is willing to respond to their material needs. God says to Moses that by such provision "you shall know that I am the Lord your God."

Second, God's responsiveness to God's people draws concrete human action into God's saturated self-revelation. The Hebrew word translated in verses 7 and 10 as "glory" in most versions of scripture connotes superabundance and surplus. It signifies God's splendor, which is so bright it is overwhelming. This is the same word Moses uses in Exod. 33:18 when he asks to see the Lord's "glory." The Lord replies that the fullness of God's self-revelation is too great for any to behold and yet live. The Lord does however reveal God's backside to Moses (33:21-23).

God's revelation doesn't just happen in Exodus 16. God gives Godself inasmuch as the people give themselves over to the Lord in faith. The people of Israel are called "to draw near" to the Lord (v. 9) and the people respond by "looking" to the Lord with a certain vision fueled by faith (v. 10). Moreover, God's provision displays God's covenantal fidelity to the Israelites and at the same time summons embodied faithfulness from the Israelites. God's provision is also a test of Israel's faithfulness to trust God and follow God's statutes (vv. 7, 28)

Third, what God gives is both material and spiritual. The Lord makes it clear to Moses that God's response to the people's cries is to "rain bread from heaven" (vv. 4, 35). There is no question left as to the *source* of God's provision (v. 12). When the people received this proof of God's faithfulness they don't know quite what to make of it. Upon seeing the bread from heaven they ask one another, "What is it?" (v. 15). Moses has to tell them that it is bread from heaven, or manna, as they came to call it (v. 31).

Even as God's provision was spiritual in origin, God *really* provided for the Israelites' physical needs: "those who gathered much had nothing over, and those who gathered little had no shortage; they gathered as much as each of them needed" (v. 18). This continued through the forty years that the Israelites wandered through the wilderness (v. 35). Wait! No leftovers for forty years! Hooray!

Fourth, that which we receive from God is at once nourishing and yet it cannot be preserved. In verse 19 we read Moses' instructions, "Don't leave any of it till the morning (v. 19). The superabundant Wor(l)d that is at once spiritual and material rots when it is not immediately consumed. When the manna was not eaten straight away "it bred worms and became foul" (v. 20). We cannot handle the truth.

The Erotic Approach, Step 3: Can't Touch This!

The Wor(l)d of God revealed in and through scripture is not a thing, object, or even a meaning. The purpose of engaging scripture oriented toward life is to see without fully seeing, to listen without fully hearing. That which we receive from God as we seek God's Wor(l)d in and through scripture is a gift. Love is what helps us see the Wor(l)d as a gift in its most radical sense.

The gift we receive in love is not a thing. You can't touch the Wor(l)d of God. We cannot seize, grasp, or steal it. It can only be given by the other. The self who receives the gift of God's self-revelation is no longer a self as subject or knower; she is a self as gifted or beloved.

Reading scripture is a paradox. As our friend Stephen Moore puts it, "The critic, while appearing to grasp the meaning of the text from a position safely outside or above it, has unknowingly been grasped by the text and pulled into it."[5] Indeed, the subject who initiates the erotic approach by seeking to love the other, to refuse to objectify the other, beyond all quest for certainty, finds himself on the other side as one claimed, named, and summoned by God to make love happen in the world. That is the purpose of scripture; it's what makes it God's *Word*, and it's what reveals God's *World*.

Thus, at the final step of the erotic approach wherein we behold the saturated Wor(l)d of God that we cannot touch, handle, or bend to our ends, we discover ourselves and our callings anew. Before God we are not subjects who objectify all that we encounter. Rather, by the erotic approach we become a witness to Love and to the Love who calls for us to make love happen in the world.

If we start to think practically about the saturated Wor(l)d, we are reduced to scratching our heads. Imagine this: I tell you that there is a sponge saturated to the point of overflowing. As soon as you take hold of the sponge, even more moisture leaks out. The desire to take hold of the waterlogged sponge leads me to lose some of the water it contained.

Moving from this mundane example to the radical superabundance of God's revelation of Godself in and through the Wor(l)d, what are we supposed to actually do? At first blush, you've already gained a positive and this can be used to reframe our engagement with scripture and neighbors. But the good thing is that when we can see God's Word as saturated, it makes it ludicrous to think we could ever claim or capture the entirety of God's Wor(l)d in a meaning, or a truth, or a social program. The point of this third step of the erotic approach is not to handle but to open yourself up to *be handled* in service to the Word, to participate in the love of God and neighbor that constitutes the World of God, or, as Jesus likes to call it, the Kingdom of God.

More Than You Can Imagine: An Example from *Tomorrowland*

That which we receive through the erotic approach, or better, that which we *might* receive—remember, there are no guarantees in love—is at once tangible and yet unhandleable (another word that ought to exist, but doesn't—not yet, anyway). You're probably wanting to say something to me right now, something like, "Hey brov, what's 'is bollocks about what can be touched but ain't to be handled?" And I respond, "Come now, my cheeky friend, did you really expect that any approach to God in the way of Jesus would be anything but paradoxical? But worry not; I have an example."

In the recent Disney film *Tomorrowland*, we find a way of thinking about the saturated Wor(l)d of God received in and through scripture by the erotic approach. The film's protagonist is Casey Newton, a teenage girl whose scientific prowess is surpassed only by her hope-filled curiosity. At a point when Casey's optimism is seeming to wane, she discovers a coin-sized orange and blue pin emblazoned with the letter T. When she touches the pin, her whole world changes. Literally.

When Casey's skin makes contact with the pin she is able to see an alternative universe teaming with scientific innovation and possibility. She later learns that this strange new world is called Tomorrowland—in case the film's title didn't tip you off. The moment Casey breaks contact with the pin she is no longer able to perceive this other world but is forced to see the world that you and I know all too well.

Casey sneaks out of bed one night resolved to learn more about this amazing new land. By intermittently touching the pin, Casey is able to move through the mundane world in route to the world revealed by the pin (the progression is akin to following a GPS in your car). As the story progresses, Casey learns that the fantastical realm of Tomorrowland is a summons to innovation and hope. It is in this way that *Tomorrowland* helps us understand the third step of the erotic approach I am forwarding.

Making love with scripture opens us up to a way of seeing the world beyond the mundane, rational mindset inaugurated by Western modernity that continues to suffuse the church with its means and methods. The Word of God opens us up to perceive the World of God, but this World is only perceivable to the one with eyes to see and ears to hear. Such a visioning and hearing is made possible beyond its empirical impossibility in and through love. It is this World that summons us to a way of being in the world that regards human and non-humans alike as more than mere objects to be handled, managed, and even marginalized in our neo-liberal economic climate. This World that we cannot handle nevertheless calls us to be handled by God in service to the other as neighbor—boldly and bodily. Such a World opened up by the Word of God destroys any possibility of ethical quietism or sociopolitical disengagement; rather, it hearkens us to the cries of the marginalized, the oppressed, and the disenfranchised, and stirs us to compassion on their behalf. Such a World is worthy of our attention.

Remembering the Future

Interpreting the Bible has frequently been compared with Jacob's experience of wrestling the angel at the river Jabbok. The idea is that we, like Jacob, must be relentless in our pursuit of biblical meaning, in spite of the pain. I believe that this analogy is false.

Biblical meaning is not something we can wrestle to the ground in order to "claim our blessing." Sheer force will not make the Word submit. Such will not deliver the World, as the harbingers of the Social Gospel Movement in American and the Christian

Social Movement in Europe learned all too well in the wake of World War I.[6]

The erotic approach requires effort on our part to be sure; but it is an effort that shares nothing with combat or fisticuffs. Our experiences with the text's numerous gaps and blockages, deadfalls and dead ends, are not in place to make it more challenging. It's not like a Tough Mudder competition. If the Bible is like a labyrinth, then it is one that was never meant to be solved. There's no truth, or answer, or governing principle waiting for us on the other side of our reading. This is why Christ-followers must never again think of the Bible according to the prosaic acronym Basic Instructions Before Leaving Earth. Hell to the no!

The Bible is not a set of operating instructions. It's not a cookbook. It is not a chemistry textbook. We cannot domesticate the Wor(l)d. We cannot leash it. Communities that hold the Bible in such esteem do not realize that on the other end of their leash rests a dragon, begging the question, who is really in control?

The Wor(l)d of God given to us in and through an erotic approach to scripture, made possible for us in its impossibility, is a certain way of seeing the world oriented to hope and attuned to human and non-human flourishing. In short, it's a way of dreaming.[7] The Wor(l)d of God harbors a call of God. This is a call that roots us in our cultural particularities and summons us back to God as a way to move forward with God in the world. It is not the recovery of a truth buried deep within the pages of scripture, but a way of discovering the truth made manifest before us when we encounter others loved by God. Such is a being-in-relation.[8]

Why Harry Potter Always Beats Voldemort: The Power of Love

To know who I am is a species of knowing where I stand.
My identity is defined by the commitments and identifications
*   which provide the . . .*
horizon within which I am capable of taking a stand.
                                        — CHARLES TAYLOR[1]

News flash: Making love with scripture is not new. In fact, it's really, really old. Ancient Christian theologians recognized the power of love as an approach to God in and through scripture, and the profundity of some of their reflections will bring tears to your eyes. St. Augustine of Hippo (b. 354 CE), for instance, said that "anyone who thinks that he has understood the divine scriptures or any part of them, but cannot by his understanding build up this double love of God and neighbor, has not yet succeeded in understanding them."[2] Likewise, St. Anselm of Canterbury (b. 1033 CE) wrote that "however strong one's faith in this supremely great reality [aka God] is, unless it lives and thrives by love, it is sterile, and is, as it were quite dead. Faith accompanied by love is not idle."[3] Love, today and yesterday, drives faith, understanding, and action.

God is love. The greatest commandment is love. The church is called to be a community of love. When we pay attention to God's theological handwriting we see that it is impossible to call yourself a Christ-follower in any sense if you do not love.

Love, we have witnessed, rises up within us out of a certain orientation toward the Word and the World. Love is a way of active listening: listening for God's Word revealed in scripture, listening for God's World revealed through scripture. Only by listening in and through scripture may we rise to the challenge of the greatest commandment. Only by loving may we participate in God's way of being and moving among us.

The Boy Who Loved

No story has captured the contemporary imagination like J. K. Rowling's seven-book masterpiece, *Harry Potter*. I confess that I am on my fifth read-through, and I am incapable of hiding my joy that my daughter has caught the magic bug much like her father has. Every night before bed she and I board the Hogwart's Express and journey into the captivating world of wizardry with Harry, Ron, and Hermione.

I believe that *Harry Potter* can help us see more clearly aspects of the erotic approach to God's Wor(l)d that we've been exploring together. The *Harry Potter* books can serve as reminders to us all as we return to scripture, giving us fresh eyes to see God's Wor(l)d. I could write a whole other book on this, and not just because I am a Hogwarts geek; however, for the sake of your patience I will restrict my reflections to four. Spoiler alert: Yeah, I'm just gonna go there; you've had your warning.

First, love marks Harry in his very flesh. We see this at several points throughout the series, but the clearest example is found in the first book, *Harry Potter and the Sorcerer's Stone*. When Harry is battling Professor Quirrell, who has been sharing his body secretly with Lord Voldemort, Harry's touch is unbearable to Quirrell. Dumbledore later explains to Harry that the reason Professor Quirrell could not touch Harry or be touched by Harry is on account of the love Harry's mother bestowed upon him when he was a baby. Dumbledore says that such a love "leaves a mark." Such a mark cannot be seen; it resides in one's flesh.

Have not we who have been grafted into God's redemptive and all-embracing love also been marked in such a way? Of course we have, and the Bible tells us that nothing can separate us from God's abiding love (Rom. 8:37-39). Moreover, just as Harry discovered when his touch destroyed Professor Quirrell, the love that abides in us can also flow through us to combat evil in the world. *Harry Potter* reminds us of the love that abides within us and the power such love can have upon a world suffused with evil, suffering, and injustice.

Second, love forms community. Love structures Harry's sense of interdependence versus Lord Voldemort's obdurate attitude of self-sufficiency. One of the central themes throughout the Harry Potter books is that Harry is not alone. How many times do we encounter the names "Harry, Ron, and Hermione" in succession? How often does Rowling tell us that Harry is surrounded by a kind of "host of witnesses" comprised of the living and the dead? The central point of difference between Harry and Voldemort is in the quality of their relationships.

To illustrate, in the final book of the series, *Harry Potter and the Deathly Hallows*, we see the Hogwarts community rally around Harry. They are willing to fight and die for Harry, which is the greatest display of love (John 15:13). By contrast, note how quickly Lord Voldemort's followers abandon him at the story's end, leaving him to face Harry alone. Moreover, Harry is prepared to die for his friends. Voldemort, on the other hand, murders Severus

Snape, one of his most faithful servants, just to get a smidge more power. Harry dies with those he loves and those who love him right beside him. Voldemort dies the way he lived his life: alone and lonely. Repeatedly, Voldemort insists that he doesn't need any help. Harry, by contrast, recognizes his need for his loved ones, that he could not be Harry without them.

Third, love drives Harry's actions in the world. Love is not just a feeling for Harry: it defines his way of being in the world. Much of the narrative drive of the Harry Potter books arises out of Harry's love for others against Lord Voldemort's evil schemes. Harry's *doing* of love displays clearly the double-edge of love: divestment and boldness. Harry repeatedly risks his own safety and comfort to protect those he loves.

In Book 2, *Harry Potter and the Chamber of Secrets*, Harry faces a basilisk (a horrific, snake-like monster), to save Ginny Weasley's life. His courage is marked by loving concern for his best friend's sister. And even when Harry is separated from Ron and Hermione, he ventures into the Chamber of Secrets alone.

We witness this again in the final book of the series as Harry makes the long walk into the Forbidden Forest to face Lord Voldemort so that nobody else will have to die. Harry displays the selflessness of love when he lays down his life for his friends. At the same time, Harry shows the courageousness of love by choosing to give up his life for his loved ones. When Harry dies, Dumbledore puts into words what we have been thinking when he says to Harry, "You wonderful boy. You brave, brave man." Harry shows us the dual nature of love.

Fourth, in the *Harry Potter* books love is the supreme form of power in the world. In Book 5, *Harry Potter and the Order of the Phoenix*, Dumbledore explains to Harry the significance of the prophecy that set all of Voldemort's sinister machinations in play. The prophecy foretold that Harry would have "power the Dark Lord knows not." Harry can't see the truth of this prophecy and so Dumbledore embarks on another of his trademark tangents, or so it seems.

Dumbledore remarks that there is a room in the Department of Mysteries that is kept locked at all times. This room contains a force that is at once wonderful and terrible, a force stronger than even death, human intelligence, and the forces of nature. Dumbledore quips that this force is the most mysterious of the many subjects for study that reside there, telling Harry, "It is the power held within that room that you possess in such quantities and which Voldemort has not at all." This force is none other than that of love.

That's the Power of Love

Power is love. Love is power. God displays God's power "in first loving us." We display our love of God, self, and neighbor by employing the power given to us as a catalyst for life and flourishing. This is what it means to *make love with scripture*.

The whole point of the Bible is to inaugurate a relationship between God, neighbor, and self defined and sustained by love. If you want to be a Christ-follower you must avoid one of two errors, and such errors are drifting further and further apart as the church wrestles with its orientation to our postmodern, postcolonial, post-Christian world.

The first error is to disregard scripture as passé. Scripture teaches us, and continues to teach us with each new reading, what love and power—what love as power—look like. If you abandon scripture reading as a practice you are like an electric car without current. You will not go far. Scripture is your power source. Likewise, if your community of faith does not commit itself to the prayerful reading of the scriptures, to preaching and teaching from the scriptures, and to works of love driven by the scriptures (1 Tim. 4:12-3), then I suggest you find another church.

The second error is to hunker down into a biblical fundamentalism that idolizes the words of scripture. There can be no storming of the gates of heaven. Biblical interpretation has nothing in common with capture the flag. God's Word cannot be seized; it can only be received in love. Furthermore, that which we do receive from God we hold as water with cupped hands—sufficient to nourish us, but unable to be contained. Biblical inerrancy and infallibility—to the degree that we can call these ideologies *biblical*—share no part of the love of God, nor do they manifest any power. They supplant God's radical freedom with human ideology deciding *in advance* what and how scripture ought to mean.

At day's end, we step out in faith. We hear Jesus' call to follow him and in so doing we embark upon the path of love. With Jesus we discover that this path is tortuous—twisting here, undulating there. And yet we ought not fear. Even as the path is love, love also illuminates the path, casting light on our neighbor who is in need. When we step into that light in love we join those saints whom God has drawn into God's very bosom—Augustine, Luther, Teresa, King, Romero, Day, and a host of others who have leaned into the way of God in Jesus Christ, which was always love.

My hope and prayer for you is that the love of God would guide you and keep you. That God's love would open you fully to human and nonhuman others. That the Wor(l)d of God revealed in and through scripture would cause love to stir up within you. And that Jesus Christ, love incarnate, would bless you as you journey with him in love.

Notes

Introduction

1. Miroslav Volf, *Exclusion & Embrace: A Theological Exploration of Identity, Otherness, and Reconciliation* (Nashville: Abingdon, 1996), 24.

2. Throughout this book, when I capitalize "Word," I am signifying God's self-revelation of Godself in the sense articulated by Swiss theologian Karl Barth. God's Word finds its fullest expression in Jesus Christ. Holy Scripture is also the Word of God inasmuch as it bears witness to God's revelation in Jesus. Lastly, Christian proclamation is also the Word of God to the degree that it bears witness to Jesus through Holy Scripture. Theology nerds—and if there were a theological galaxy, Barth would be in contention for the title "Grand Nerd Overlord"—refer to this as the "threefold Word of God." See Karl Barth, *Church Dogmatics* I/1, ed. T. F. Torrance, trans. G. W. Bromiley (Edinburgh: T. & T. Clark, 1975), §4.

3. For more on what I mean by "mainstream" (aka "malestream") interpretations, see Elisabeth Schüssler Fiorenza, *Jesus and the Politics of Interpretation* (New York: Continuum, 2001) and idem, *Rhetoric and Ethic: The Politics of Biblical Studies* (Minneapolis: Augsburg Fortress, 1999).

4. Gustavo Gutiérrez, "Toward a Theology of Liberation," in *Gustavo Gutiérrez: Essential Writings*, ed. James B. Nickoloff (Maryknoll, NY: Orbis, 1996), 24.

5. See Ps. 111:10; Prov. 1:7; and 1 John 4:8.

6. In a letter written to an influential pagan leader named Volusian, Augustine wrote of "the manifold darkness of mystery" and "a depth of wisdom lying hidden" in Holy Scripture that remains beyond even "the most advanced in years, the most penetrating in mind, the most ardent in zeal for learning." (Augustine, "*Ep.* 137.1.3," in *Fathers of the Church: Saint Augustine Letters*, vol. 3,

trans. Sister Wilfrid Parsons (Washington D.C.: Catholic University of America Press, 1953), 20. Later in the letter Augustine writes, "The very language in which Holy Scripture is woven is accessible to all, though very, very few penetrate it. In its easily understood parts it speaks to the heart of the unlearned and the learned like a familiar friend who uses no guile, but in those truths that it veils in mystery, it does not raise itself aloft with proud speech. Hence, the backward and untutored mind dares to draw near to it as a poor man to a rich one, because it invites all in simple language and feeds their minds with its teaching in plain words, while training them in the truth by its hidden message, having the same affect in both the obvious and the obscure."

7. Michel Foucault, *The Birth of the Clinic*, trans. Alan Sheridan (London: Rutledge, 1989), xvii–xviii: "We are doomed historically to history, to the patient construction of discourses about discourses, and to the task of hearing what has already been said. But is it inevitable that we should know of no other function for speech (*parole*) than that of commentary? *Commentary* questions discourse as to what it says and intended to say; it tries to uncover that deeper meaning of speech that enables it to achieve an identity with itself, supposedly nearer to its essential truth; in other words, in stating what has been said, one has to re-state what has never been said."

Chapter 1

1. Mayra Rivera, *The Touch of Transcendence: A Postcolonial Theology of God* (Louisville: Westminster John Knox, 2007), 47.

2. Karl Barth, "The Christian's Place in Society," in *The Word of God and the Word of Man*, trans. Douglas Horton (Gloucester, MA: Peter Smith, 1978), 282–83.

3. Origen, *On First Principles*, trans. G. W. Butterworth (Gloucester, MA: Peter Smith, 1973), IV:2:8.

4. Jean-Luc Marion, "The Intentionality of Love," in *Prolegomena to Charity*, trans. Stephen E. Lewis (New York: Fordham University Press, 2002), 71.

5. The most common rendering of the Greek verb *gennaó* into English is "to beget." This verse is often translated "whoever loves is born of God." Obviously this is a metaphor. In a more Jewish sense, however, this verb is associated with drawing another into his way of life. Love makes us like God.

6. This is where I take issue with certain theologies that move away from God's self-revelation in Jesus to the "community of wo/men" or a "sense of unity with the natural world" as in Schüssler Fiorenza, *Jesus: Miriam's Child, Sophia's Prophet* (New York: Crossroad, 1994), 3 and Sallie McFague, *Life Abundant* (Minneapolis: Fortress Press, 2000), 136. Rather, I believe that critical theologies wide awake to God's revelation of Godself in scripture *and* life are the way to go. This requires imagination beyond the confines of Western thought,

beyond, for example the following kind of theological construction: "*So then we find our sacred power neither 'in' Jesus nor 'in' ourselves but between and among us.*" Carter Heyward, *Saving Jesus from Those Who Are Right: Rethinking What It Means to Be Christian* (Minneapolis: Fortress Press, 1999), 61.

7. See Jon Sobrino, *Spirituality of Liberation: Toward Political Holiness*, trans. Robert R. Barr (Maryknoll, NY: Orbis, 1988).

8. See Plato, *Republic*, trans. Paul Shorey (Cambridge, MA: Harvard University Press, 1930), Bk. II, 379 a, p. 182. Plato, speaking to Adeimantus, describes theology as that which arises from the ancient poets about the gods (*contra* philosophy, which gets at the true essence of things). Few Christian theologians would subscribe to Plato's conclusion: "[god] is the author of only a small part of human affairs . . . the good things we must ascribe to no other than god, while we must seek elsewhere, and not in him [*sic*], the causes of the harmful things" (379 c). Aristotle, in a derisive tone, challenges the *theologoi* (whom Tredennick curiously translates as "cosmologists") vis-à-vis his own philosophical account for metaphysics. See Aristotle, *Metaphysics*, trans. H. Tredennick (Cambridge, MA: Harvard University Press, 1935), Bk. XII, 1071 b 27, p. 142.

9. See Michel Foucault, *Technologies of the Self: A Seminar with Michel Foucault*, ed. Luther H. Martin et al. (Boston: University of Massachusetts Press, 1988), 22: "To summarize: There has been an inversion between the hierarchy of the two principles of antiquity, 'Take care of yourself' and 'Know thyself.' In Greco-Roman culture knowledge of oneself appeared as the consequence of taking care of yourself. In the modern world, knowledge of oneself constitutes the fundamental principle." See also Charles Taylor, *Sources of the Self: The Making of the Modern Identity* (Cambridge and New York: Cambridge University Press, 1989), esp. 139–58 for a historical development of the self through Western thought.

10. Simone de Beauvoir, *The Second Sex*, trans. Constance Borde and Sheila Malovany-Chevallier (New York: Vintage, 2011), 6.

11. Here I mark the existence of the Word beyond being. To say that God *is* is to reduce God to the realm of being. See Jean-Luc Marion, *God Without Being: Hors-Texte*, trans. Thomas A. Carlson (Chicago and London: University of Chicago Press, 1995). On the use of the descriptor "wholly other," my thoughts are guided by Steven G. Smith, *Argument to the Other: Reason Beyond Reason in the Thought of Karl Barth and Emmanuel Levinas*, American Academy of Religion Academy Series, No. 42 (Chino, CA: Scholars Press, 1983), 42: "Barth's argument is not that God *is* the Wholly Other. Such a statement, like any other direct theological predication, cannot stand before God. Barth's point is that *we* must speak of God *as* the Wholly Other because of the actual position in which we find ourselves, in the light of revelation."

12. See Willie James Jennings, *The Christian Imagination: Theology and the Origins of Race* (New Haven: Yale University Press, 2011).

Part 1

1. Kwok Pui-lan, "Discovering the Bible in the Non-Biblical World," *Semia* 47 (1989): 26.

2. One reviewer of the book said this in the first line of her review for *The Atlantic*: "Look, I'm not afraid to say it: *50 Shades of Grey* is a terrible book." It only gets more critical from there. Jen Doll, "The Alleged Sexiness of '50 Shades of Grey,'" *The Wire: News from the Atlantic* (May 22, 2012), http://www.thewire.com/entertainment/2012/05/alleged-sexiness-50-shades-grey/52667/. See also the movie review, Emma Green, "Consent Isn't Enough: The Troubling Sex of *Fifty Shades*," *The Atlantic* (February 10, 2015), http://www.theatlantic.com/features/archive/2015/02/consent-isnt-enough-in-fifty-shades-of-grey/385267/.

3. Let me drop a footnote here to make something absolutely clear. It is *not* the case that for 1900 years there was this singular way of reading scripture. History bears witness to the cries of the oppressed smothered by the pillow of totalization. For instance, numerous Catholic priests of various orders stood in solidarity with the oppressed Taino Indians and Native Americans *at the same time* that other priests were wielding theology and scripture to subjugate the so-called "savages."

Chapter 2

1. Jean-Louis Chrétien, *Under the Gaze of the Bible*, trans. John Marson Dunaway (New York: Fordham University Press, 2015), 3.

2. Stanley Fish, *Is There a Text in This Class? The Authority of Interpretive Communities* (Cambridge, MA and London: Harvard University Press, 1980), 7.

3. In this chapter I am especially indebted to the following essays: Georges Poulet, "Phenomenology of Reading," *New Literary History* 1, no. 1 (1969): 53–68; Roland Barthes, "The Death of the Author," in *Image, Music, Text*, trans. Stephen Heath (New York: Noonday, 1988), 142–64; and Michel Foucault, "What Is an Author?," in *The Foucault Reader*, ed. Paul Rabinow, trans. Josué V. Harari (New York: Pantheon, 1984), 101–20.

4. Hans-Georg Gadamer, *Truth and Method*, rev. edition, trans. Joel Weinsheimer and Donald G. Marshall (New York and London: Continuum, 2004), 306, 374–79.

5. Foucault, "What Is an Author?," 101.

6. Barthes, "The Death of the Author," 148.

7. Foucault, "What Is an Author?," 119.

Chapter 3

1. Avery Dulles, *Models of Revelation* (Garden City, NY: Doubleday, 1983), 209.

2. See Willie Jennings, *The Christian Imagination: Theology and the Origins of Race* (New Haven and London: Yale University Press, 2010).

3. Shawn Carter, *Decoded* (New York: Random House, 2010), 57. By the way, Jay Z states that the "bitch" to which his song refers is not a derogatory reference to women, but an allusion to the drug dog, the dog that never showed up, and if it had, the artist we know as Jay Z might still be in jail.

4. See Cornel West, *Prophesy Deliverance!* anniversary edition (Louisville: Westminster John Knox, 2002).

5. Stanley Fish, *Is There a Text in This Class? The Authority of Interpretive Communities* (Cambridge, MA: Harvard University Press, 1982), 322: "[M]eanings are the property neither of fixed and stable texts nor of free and independent readers but of interpretive communities that are responsible both for the shape of the readers' activities and for the texts those activities produce."

6. Brian K. Blount, *Cultural Interpretation: Reorienting New Testament Criticism* (Minneapolis: Fortress Press, 1995), 176.

7. Fernando F. Segovia, "Criticism in Critical Times: Reflections on Vision and Task," *Journal of Biblical Literature* 134, no. 1 (2015): 27, 29.

8. Wil Gafney, "A Queer Womanist Midrashic Reading of Numbers 25:1-8," in *Leviticus and Numbers*, ed. Athalya Brenner and Archie Chi Chung (Minneapolis: Fortress Press, 2013), writes, "In any interpretive framework, this is a queer—in every sense of the word—text" (191).

9. Furthermore, none see this as a show of hospitality. See, for example, Martin Noth, *Numbers: A Commentary*, Old Testament Library, trans. James D. Martin (London: SCM, 1968), 196–98; Baruch A. Levine, *Numbers 21-36: A New Translation*, Anchor Yale Bible Commentary (New York: Random House, 2000), 295–97.

10. In another essay, she writes that her "primary self-designation is as a black feminist," but that she often articulates a hybridized identity as a fem/womanist. Wilda C. M. Gafney, "A Black Feminist Approach to Biblical Studies," *Encounter* 67, no. 4 (2006): 397.

11. See Num. 31:18; Deut. 20:14; 21:10-17; Judg. 21:10-12.

12. Gafney writes, "I also suggest that the Israelite and Moabite gods were not viewed as polemically opposed by their worshipers as they were by the framers and many interpreters of the text" ("A Queer Womanist Midrashic Reading," 193).

13. Justo L. González, *Santa Biblia: The Bible Through Hispanic Eyes* (Nashville: Abingdon, 1996), 62.

14. The reaction in Latin@ communities, González notes, "is not one of mystification and outrage, as in a middle-class congregation, but rather of joy and celebration" (63).

15. González, *Santa Biblia*, 63.

16. Brad R. Braxton, *No Longer Slaves: Galatians and African American Experience* (Collegeville, MN: Liturgical, 2002).

17. Braxton, *No Longer Slaves*, 94.

18. Ibid., 95–96.

19. A technical way of talking about this is presented and described by A. K. M. Adam, "Integral and Differential Hermeneutics," in *The Meanings We Choose: Hermeneutical Ethics, Indeterminacy and the Conflict of Interpretations*, ed. Charles H. Cosgrove (London and New York: T. & T. Clark, 2004), 24–38. I am indebted to his helpful insights.

20. Tony Jones, *Did God Kill Jesus? Searching for Love in History's Most Famous Execution* (New York: HarperOne, 2015), 24.

Chapter 4

1. Howard Thurman, *Jesus and the Disinherited* (Boston: Beacon, 1976), 28.

2. John D. Caputo, *The Prayers and Tears of Jacques Derrida: Religion Without Religion* (Bloomington and Indianapolis: Indiana University Press, 1997), 109.

3. Elsa Tamez, "Women's Rereading of the Bible," in *Voices from the Margin: Interpreting the Bible in the Third World*, ed. R. S. Sugirtharajah, 2nd edition (London: SPCK; Maryknoll, NY: Orbis, 1995), 55. See also idem, *Bible of the Oppressed*, trans. Matthew J. O'Connell (Eugene, OR: Wipf & Stock, 2006).

4. Miguel A. De La Torre, *Liberation Theology for Armchair Theologians* (Louisville: Westminster John Knox, 2013), 19.

5. James H. Cone, *A Black Theology of Liberation*, 40th anniversary edition (Maryknoll, NY: Orbis, 2010), 32–33. See also Michael Joseph Brown, "Black Theology and the Bible," in *The Cambridge Companion to Black Theology* (Cambridge: Cambridge University Press, 2012), 169–83. I should note that the adamancy of most liberation theologies on the centrality of scripture persists in a tensive relationship with postcolonial theologies, which stress the emancipatory ambivalence of the Bible and the complicity of scripture in regard to empire.

6. Gustavo Gutiérrez, *The Power of the Poor in History*, trans. Robert R. Barr (Maryknoll, NY: Orbis, 1983), 61.

7. See Mary Daly, *The Church and the Second Sex* (Boston: Beacon, 1985 [1968]); idem, *Beyond God the Father: Toward a Philosophy of Women's Liberation* (Boston: Beacon, 1973); idem, *Gyn/ecology: The Metaethics of Radical Feminism* (Boston: Beacon, 1978); Rosemary Radford Ruether, *Sexism and God-Talk: Toward a Feminist Theology*, 10th anniversary edition (Boston: Beacon, 1993); idem, *Womanguides: Readings Toward a Feminist Theology* (Boston: Beacon, 1985); and idem, *New Woman, New Earth: Sexist Ideologies and Human Liberation* (New York: Seabury, 1975).

8. Elisabeth Schüssler Fiorenza, *In Memory of Her* (New York: Crossroad, 1986), 35.

9. Elizabeth A. Johnson, *She Who Is: The Mystery of God in Feminist Theological Discourse* (New York: Crossroad, 1993), 77: "A certain cast of mind arises which holds that this male terminology for God is in a particular way 'revealed' and must continue to predominate. 'Revelation' then becomes a brake on the articulation of divine mystery in the light of women's dignity."

10. See Matt. 16:24. "The option for the poor derives simply from the fact that the poor are the abandoned, the marginalized of a society such as we know it; and therefore God makes an option for them, in order to bestow the reign upon them. This is the understanding of the gospel that we adopt." Juan Luis Segundo, *Signs of the Times: Theological Reflections*, ed. Alfred T. Hennely, S.J., trans. Robert R. Barr (Maryknoll, NY: Orbis, 1993), 121.

11. Leonardo Boff and Clodovis Boff, *Introducing Liberation Theology*, trans. Paul Burns (Maryknoll, NY: Orbis, 1987), 22.

12. Church historian and theologian Justo L. González, *Santa Biblia: The Bible Through Hispanic Eyes* (Nashville: Abingdon, 1996), writes that for many poor Latinos the scriptures are not read primarily for guidance or for information, but rather for insight and strength. "When the poor read the Bible, they do not find there a blueprint for escaping their poverty . . . what they find is rather a worldview, and an interpretation of their own predicament, that put things under a new light and give them a new sense of worth and of hope."

13. Ada María Isasi-Díaz, "Introduction," in *La Lucha Continues: Mujerista Theology* (Maryknoll, NY: Orbis, 2004), 3.

14. Ada María Isasi-Díaz, "*Mujerista* Theology: A Challenge to Traditional Theology," in *Mujerista Theology: A Theology for the Twenty-first Century* (Maryknoll, NY: Orbis, 1996), 60.

15. Ada María Isasi-Díaz, "La Palabra de Dios en Nosotros: The Word of God in Us," in *Searching the Scriptures*, vol. 1, ed. Elisabeth Schüssler Fiorenza (New York: Crossroad, 1993), 87.

16. Isasi-Díaz, "La Palabra de Dios en Nosotros," 89.

17. See Jacqueline M. Hidalgo, "Reading from No Place: Toward a Hybrid and Ambivalent Study of Scriptures," in *Latino/a Biblical Hermeneutics: Problematics, Objectives, Strategies*, ed. Francisco Lozada and Fernando Segovia (Atlanta: Society of Biblical Literature, 2014), 165–86.

18. Nancy Cardosa Pereira, "Commodity Aesthetics and the Erotics of Relationship: Challenges of Feminist Hermeneutics of Liberation to Market Aesthetics," trans. Thia Cooper, in *Liberation Theology and Sexuality*, ed. Marcella Althaus-Reid (Aldershot, UK and Burlington, VT: Ashgate, 2006), 77.

19. Dwight N. Hopkins, *Being Human: Race, Culture, and Religion* (Minneapolis: Fortress Press, 2005), 129. He argues that contemporary theological

discourse "must take on the discourse of race because God interacts with human beings through culture in specific collective selves and the individual self."

20. Cone, *A Black Theology of Liberation*, 30.

21. James H. Cone, *Black Theology and Black Power*, updated and expanded edition (Maryknoll, NY: Orbis, 1997), 8. Cone writes, "This is Black Power, the power of a black man to say Yes to his own 'black being,' and to make the other accept him or be prepared for a struggle."

22. James H. Cone, *God of the Oppressed* (Maryknoll, NY: Orbis, 1997), 32: "Jesus Christ is the subject of Black Theology because he is the content of the hopes and dreams of black people."

23. Vincent L. Wimbush, "Reading Texts as Reading Ourselves: A Chapter in the History of African-American Biblical Interpretation," in *Reading from This Place*, vol. 1, Social Location and Biblical Interpretation in the United States, ed. Fernando F. Segovia and Mary Ann Tolbert (Minneapolis: Fortress Press, 1995), 103.

24. Vincent L. Wimbush, *White Men's Magic: Scripturalization as Slavery* (Oxford: Oxford University Press, 2014), 87.

25. As one prominent womanist theologian once put it, "Feminist theology is inadequate for two reasons: it is *White* and *racist*." Jacquelyn Grant, *White Women's Christ and Black Women's Jesus: Feminist Christology and Womanist Response* (Atlanta: Scholars, 1989), 195.

26. Such readings, however, are fraught with challenges. Weems writes, "The African American female reader, in essence, finds herself permanently reading as an outsider as long as she is unwilling and incapable to deal creatively in partitioning out her double identity as woman and African American" (Renita J. Weems, "Reading Her Way Through the Struggle: African American Women and the Bible," in *Stony the Road We Trod: African American Biblical Interpretation*, ed. Cain Hope Felder [Minneapolis: Fortress Press, 1991], 68).

27. bell hooks, *Talking Back: Thinking Feminist, Thinking Black* (Boston: South End, 1989), 78. See also Audre Lorde, "Eye to Eye: Black Woman, Hatred, and Anger," in *Sister Outsider* (New York: Crossing, 1984), 146–47.

28. hooks, *Talking Back*, 9.

29. Patricia L. Hunter makes the following claim: "What is critical for Christian women of color is to understand the contradiction of believing all of creation is good (including women of color) while treating ourselves as less than acceptable to God, and accepting despicable treatment from men and other women." "Women's Power—Women's Passion," in *A Troubling in My Soul: Womanist Perspectives on Evil & Suffering*, ed. Emilie M. Townes (Maryknoll, NY: Orbis, 1993), 190.

30. Weems, "Reading Her Way," 59.

31. Brian K. Blount, *Cultural Interpretation: Reorienting New Testament Criticism* (Minneapolis: Fortress Press, 1995), 183.

32. Those of you keeping score at home will note that there is much that I left out of this chapter. I failed to attend to emerging theologies and hermeneutics of migrant, diaspora, and intercultural readings of the Bible, which blur the onto-logical and epistemological boundaries this chapter presents. Moreover, among many others, I said nothing about Native American, Oceanic, Aboriginal, or disability theologies of scripture. Furthermore, many readers will observe that I give attention to those canonical voices within their respective arenas of inquiry. All of these theologians held/hold prominent positions within the theological academy at some of the top universities and seminaries in the world. Thus, I did not control for education and economic conditions that also shape these writers' respective theologies. Please note, my dear reader, that these omissions result from word count constraints rather than a devaluing of these communities and interpretations on my part. See Jean-Pierre Ruiz, *Readings from the Edges: The Bible for People on the Move* (Maryknoll, NY: Orbis, 2011) and the essays in *Interpreting Beyond Borders*, The Bible and Postcolonialism, vol. 3, ed. Fernando F. Segovia (Sheffield: Sheffield Academic Press, 2000) and *Through the Eyes of Another: Intercultural Readings of the Bible*, ed. Hans de Wit et al. (Nappanee, IN: Institute of Mennonite Studies and Vrije Universiteit, Amsterdam, 2004). See also Clara Kidwell, Homer Noley, and George Tinker, *A Native American Theology* (Maryknoll, NY: Orbis, 2001); Jione Havea, David Neville, and Elaine E. Wainwright, eds., *Bible, Borders, Belonging(s): Engaging Readings from Ocea-nia* (Atlanta: Society of Biblical Literature, 2014); Garry W. Trompf, ed., *The Gospel Is Not Western: Black Theologies of the Southwest Pacific* (Maryknoll, NY: Orbis, 1987); Anne Pattel-Gray, "Methodology in an Aboriginal Theology," in *The Cambridge Companion to Black Theology*, ed. Dwight N. Hopkins and Edward P. Antonio (Cambridge: Cambridge University Press, 2012), 278–97; and Nancy L. Eiesland, *The Disabled God: Toward a Liberatory Theology of Dis-ability* (Nashville: Abingdon, 1994).

Part II

1. Jacques Derrida, *Dissemination*, trans. Barbara Johnson (Chicago and London: University of Chicago Press, 1981), 63 (translation modified).

Chapter 5

1. Mark C. Taylor, *Erring: A Postmodern A/theology* (Chicago and London: University of Chicago Press, 1984), 18.

2. In his essay, "The Ends of Man," in *Margins of Philosophy*, trans. Alan Bass (Chicago: University of Chicago Press, 1982), 134–35, Derrida differentiates between a *trembling* and a *radical trembling*: "A radical trembling can only come from the *outside*. Therefore, the trembling of which I speak derives no more than any other from some spontaneous decision or philosophical thought after some internal maturation of its history." In an interview, Jacques Derrida was asked what was the most widely held misconception about his work. Derrida replied, "That I'm a skeptical nihilist who doesn't believe in anything, who thinks nothing has meaning. That's stupid and utterly wrong and only the people who haven't read me say this. This misreading of my work began 35 years ago and it's very difficult to destroy. I never said everything is linguistic and we're enclosed in language. In fact, I say the opposite, and the deconstruction of logo-centrism was conceived to dismantle precisely this philosophy for which everything is language. Anyone who reads my work with attention understands that I insist on affirmation and faith, and that I'm full of respect for the texts I read." Kirby Dick and Amy Ziering Kofman, *Derrida: Screenplay and Essays of the Film* (London: Routledge, 2005), 120–21.

3. Karl Barth, *The Epistle to the Romans*, 6th edition, trans. Edwyn C. Hoskyns (London, Oxford, and New York: Oxford University Press, 1933), 123: "[Faith is] the impossibility from which all possibility emerges, the miracle from which proceeds all human experience, the paradox by which all direct and visible human being and having and doing is limited and rendered questionable— and is established and affirmed . . . that he heard the 'No' of God and understood it as His 'Yes'—this is Abraham's faith."

4. Jacques Derrida, "Letter to a Japanese Friend," in *A Derrida Reader: Between the Blinds*, ed. Peggy Kamuf, trans. David Wood and Andrew Benjamin (New York: Columbia University Press, 1991), 274: "Deconstruction takes place, it is an event that does not await the deliberation, consciousness, or organization of a subject, or even of modernity. It deconstructs itself."

5. Jacques Derrida, *Memoires for Paul de Man*, trans. Cecile Lindsay, Jonathan Culler, and Eduardo Cadava (New York: Columbia University Press, 1986), 73: "The disruptive force of deconstruction is always already contained within the architecture of the work."

Chapter 6

1. Elaine Scarry, "The Interior Structure of Made Objects," in *The Postmodern Bible Reader*, ed. David Jobling, Tina Pippin, and Ronald Schleifer (Oxford and Malden, MA: Blackwell, 2001), 290.

2. One of the most influential and compelling exemplars of radical readings of scripture is New Testament scholar Stephen Moore. He explains that

there are really two "waves" of poststructural deconstruction in American contexts. The "first wave" was primarily focused with the intricate inner workings of literary texts, attending in particular to the ways in which deconstruction is always already at work within these texts. The "second wave," arising in the mid-1980s, was primarily preoccupied with the intricate relations of literary texts to other social and cultural realia, not least gender/sexuality, race/ethnicity, and colonialism/postcolonialism. Stephen D. Moore, *The Bible in Theory: Critical and Postcritical Essays* (Atlanta: Society of Biblical Literature, 2010), 81–82.

3. Danna Nolan Fewell, "Building Babel," in *Postmodern Interpretations of the Bible: A Reader*, ed. A. K. M. Adam (St. Louis: Chalice, 2001), 3.

4. Fewell, "Building Babel," 12.

5. Ibid., 15.

6. She labels this "the racialization of nonheteronormativity." Erin Runions, "From Disgust to Humor: Rahab's Queer Affect," in *Bible Trouble: Queering Reading at the Boundaries of Biblical Scholarship*, ed. Teresa J. Hornsby and Ken Stone (Atlanta: Society of Biblical Literature, 2011), 45.

7. See Marcella Althaus-Reid, "Searching for a Queer Sophia-Wisdom: The Postcolonial Rahab," in *Patriarchs, Prophets and Other Villains*, ed. Lisa Isherwood (London: Equinox, 2007), 128–40; and Ken Stone, "Queering the Canaanite," in *The Sexual Theologian: Essays on Sex, God, and Politics*, ed. Marcella Althaus-Reid and Lisa Isherwood (London: T. & T. Clark, 2004), 110–34.

8. Runions, "From Disgust to Humor," 63.

9. Ibid., 66.

10. Ibid., 70.

11. Stephen D. Moore, "Are There Impurities in the Living Water That the Johannine Jesus Dispenses? Deconstruction, Feminism, and the Samaritan Woman," in *The Bible in Theory*, 81–97.

12. Moore, *The Bible in Theory*, 87.

13. And here a real problem is presented to interpreters. None have been able to locate the whence of this scripture reference that Jesus cites, neither in the Masoretic (Hebrew) Text nor in the Septuagint (the Greek translation of the Old Testament). What then is the actual *source* of the living water? Jesus or the believer? The Fourth Gospel or some other source that is lost to us?

14. "Tracing the water imagery upstream, therefore, we arrive at its apparent source. Contrary to what one might expect, Jesus himself is not that source. The stream does not issue from Jesus' presence; rather, it is from Jesus' *absence* that it flows. . . . And absence is the source of desire. The water imagery in John is a river of desire, then; it issues from the Fourth Evangelist, although it cannot be said to have originated with him" (96).

Chapter 7

1. Luce Irigaray, *To Speak Is Never Neutral*, trans. Gail Schwab (London: Routledge, 2002), 4.

2. John D. Caputo, *The Insistence of God: A Theology of Perhaps* (Bloomington and Indianapolis: Indiana University Press, 2013), 63: "The 'radical' in radical theology goes to the roots of classical theology and uproots them, pulling up by the root the *logos* of the old theology and replacing it with a poetics."

3. R. S. Sugirtharajah, "Convergent Trajectories? Liberation Hermeneutics and Postcolonial Biblical Criticism," in *Postcolonial Criticism and Biblical Interpretation* (New York: Oxford University Press, 2002), 101.

4. At this point of critique, postcolonial theologies of scripture overlap with liberation theologies of scripture, their methodological differences notwithstanding. See Mayra Rivera and Stephen D. Moore, "A Tentative Topography of Postcolonial Theology," in *Planetary Loves: Spivak, Postcoloniality, and Theology*, ed. Stephen D. Moore (New York: Fordham University Press, 2010), 8.

5. Musa W. Dube, *Postcolonial Feminist Interpretation of the Bible* (St. Louis: Chalice, 2000), 17.

6. Catherine Keller, Michael Nausner, and Mayra Rivera, "Introduction: Alien/Nation, Liberation, and the Postcolonial Underground," in *Postcolonial Theologies: Divinity and Empire* (St. Louis: Chalice, 2004), 12.

7. See R. S. Sugirtharajah, *The Bible and Asia: From the Pre-Christian Era to the Postcolonial Age* (Cambridge, MA: Harvard University Press, 2013); idem, *Exploring Postcolonial Biblical Criticism: History, Method, Practice* (Oxford: Wiley-Blackwell, 2012); idem, *Troublesome Texts: The Bible in Colonial and Contemporary Culture* (Sheffield: Phoenix, 2008); idem, *The Bible and Empire: Postcolonial Explorations* (Cambridge: Cambridge University Press, 2005); idem, *Postcolonial Reconfigurations: An Alternative Way of Reading the Bible and Doing Theology* (London: SCM, 2003); idem, *Postcolonial Criticism and Biblical Interpretation* (Oxford: Oxford University Press, 2002); idem, *The Bible and the Third World: Precolonial, Colonial and Postcolonial Encounters* (Cambridge: Cambridge University Press, 2001); and idem, *Asian Biblical Hermeneutics and Postcolonialism: Contesting the Interpretations* (Maryknoll, NY: Orbis, 1998).

8. Kwok Pui-lan, *Postcolonial Imagination & Feminist Theology* (Louisville: Westminster John Knox, 2005), 144.

9. Stephen D. Moore, *God's Beauty Parlor: And Other Queer Spaces in and Around the Bible* (Stanford: Stanford University Press, 2001), 18. Moore and others use the singular *queer theory* with some reservation, and I continue with the same trepidation.

10. Elizabeth Stuart, *Gay and Lesbian Theologies: Repetitions with Critical Difference* (Aldershot, UK and Burlington, VT: Ashgate, 2003), 89.

11. Patrick S. Cheng writes about boundary-breaking love in his book *Radical Love: An Introduction to Queer Theory* (New York: Seabury, 2011), 45.

12. Stuart, *Gay and Lesbian Theologies*, 83. This orientation toward liberation is not universally shared, but it is still one of the most common foci for queer theologies. Cf. Gavin D'Costa, "Queer Trinity," in *Queer Theology: Rethinking the Western Body*, ed. Gerard Loughlin (Oxford and Malden, MA: Blackwell, 2007), 270: "[T]he aims of certain queer theorists have been overtly ideological: to 'liberate' gay men or lesbian women or bisexuals or transgendered (*sic*) persons. My concern is different . . ."

13. John D. Caputo, *More Radical Hermeneutics: On Not Knowing Who We Are* (Bloomington and Indianapolis: Indiana University Press, 2000), 2.

14. John D. Caputo, *What Would Jesus Deconstruct? The Good News of Postmodernism for the Church* (Grand Rapids: Baker Academic, 2007), 26.

15. Richard Kearney, *The Poetics of Imagining: Modern to Postmodern* (New York: Fordham University Press, 1998), 52, 97, 167, 243.

16. John D. Caputo, *The Weakness of God: A Theology of the Event* (Bloomington: Indiana University Press, 2006), 103–4.

17. John B. Cobb Jr. *Sustainability: Economics, Ecology, and Justice* (Maryknoll, NY: Orbis, 1992), 82.

18. Sallie McFague, *The Body of God: An Ecological Theology* (Minneapolis: Fortress Press, 1993), viii; idem, *A New Climate for Theology: God, the World, and Global Warming* (Minneapolis: Fortress Press, 2008), 113.

19. Alirio Cáceres Aguirre, "Eco-theology: Epistemological Approaches," in *Eco-Theology*, ed. Elaine Wainwright, Luiz Carlos Susin, and Felix Wilfred (London: SCM, 2009), 60.

20. Sallie McFague, *Blessed Are the Consumers: Climate Change and the Practice of Restraint* (Minneapolis: Fortress Press, 2013), 147.

21. The Earth Bible Team, "Guiding Ecojustice Principles," in *Readings from the Perspective of Earth*, The Earth Bible, vol. 1, ed. Norman C. Habel (Sheffield/Cleveland: Sheffield Academic/Pilgrim, 2000), 34–35. See also idem, "Ecojustice Hermeneutics: Reflections and Challenges," in *The Earth Story in the New Testament*, The Earth Bible, vol. 5, ed. Norman C. Habel and Vicki Balabanski (London and New York/Cleveland: Sheffield Academic/Pilgrim, 2002), 1–14.

22. Frantz Fanon, *The Wretched of the Earth*, trans. Constance Farrington (New York: Grove Weidenfeld, 1963), 7.

23. Richard Kearney, *Anatheism: Returning to God after God* (New York: Columbia University Press, 2011), 166, 167.

Part III

1. Jean-Luc Marion, *God Without Being: Hors-Texte*, trans. Thomas A. Carlson (Chicago and London: University of Chicago Press, 1991), 49.

2. As Max Scheler puts it, we must extricate ourselves from the "continuous chain of acts of revenge" and from that "secret resentment [which] underlies every way of thinking which attributes creative power to mere *negation* and *criticism*." *On Feeling, Knowing, and Valuing* (Chicago: University of Chicago Press, 1993), 132, cited in Richard Kearney, *Anatheism: Returning to God after God* (New York: Columbia University Press, 2011), 168.

3. See Audre Lorde, "Uses of Anger," in *Sister Outsider: Essays and Speeches* (New York: Crossing, 2007), 129: "Anger is an appropriate reaction to racist attitudes, as is fury when the actions arising from those attitudes do not change."

4. Much of my thinking in this regard is indebted to the careful work of Jean-Luc Marion. See Marion, "The Intentionality of Love"; idem, "What Love Knows," in *Prolegomena to Charity*, trans. Stephen E. Lewis (New York: Fordham University Press, 2002); and *The Erotic Phenomenon* (Chicago: University of Chicago Press, 2008).

5. Mike Yaconelli, *Messy Spirituality* (Grand Rapids: Zondervan, 2002), 104. He goes on to write, "Sameness is a virus that infects members of industrialized nations and causes an allergic reaction to anyone who is different."

6. In her essay "Uses of the Erotic," poet/activist Audre Lorde writes, "We have often turned away from the exploration and consideration of the erotic as a source of power and information, confusing it with its opposite, the pornographic." Audre Lorde, "Uses of the Erotic: The Erotic as Power," in *Sister Outsider*, 54.

7. See Augustine, *De vera religione* XLVI, 89, cited in Werner G. Jeanrond, *A Theology of Love* (London and New York: T. & T. Clark, 2010), 55, and Bernard of Clairvaux, *On Loving God*, trans. Robert Walton, OSB (Collegeville, MN: Cistercian, 2009).

8. See James Barr, "Words for Love in Biblical Greek," in *The Glory of Christ in the New Testament: Studies in Christology in Memory of George Bradford Caird*, ed. L. D. Hurst and N. T. Wright (Oxford: Clarendon, 1987), 3–18. The sixth-century mystical theologian Pseudo-Dionysius is often charged with supplanting the biblical notion of *agapē* with the Greek notion of *erōs*. What is clear when one pays close attention to Dionysius' writings, however, is that Dionysius employs both words to describe the Divine Love. He argues that just as "four" is equivalent to "twice two," so ought we realize that *agapē* and *erōs* are "equivalent." Pseudo-Dionysius, *Divine Names*, in *Pseudo-Dionysius: The Complete Works*, trans. Colm Luibheid and Paul Rorem (New York: Paulist, 1987),

4.10 709B. He continues, "To those listening properly to the divine things the name 'love' (*agapē*) is used by the sacred writers in divine revelation with the exact same meaning as the term 'yearning' (*erōs*)." *Divine Names*, 4.12 709C.

Chapter 8

1. Willie James Jennings, *The Christian Imagination: Theology and the Origins of Race* (New Haven: Yale University Press, 2011), 263.

2. Descartes omitted the modalities of love and hate from his definition of the *ego*: "I am a thinking thing, who doubts, affirms, denies, who understands little, is ignorant of much, who wills, who does not will, who imagines and also feels." Descartes, *Oeuvres de Descartes*, ed. C. Adam and P. Tannery, Nouvelle presentation, vol. VII (Paris: Vrin, 1964–76), 34, cited in Marion, *The Erotic Phenomenon*, 6.

3. See Karl Barth, *The Göttingen Dogmatics: Instruction in the Christian Religion*, vol. 1, ed. Hannelotte Reiffen, trans. Geoffrey W. Bromiley (Grand Rapids: Eerdmans, 1991), 327: "God's deity or person is never a mere object, never merely His being an It or a He but rather His being an I. In His revelation, precisely in His revelation, God is an irremovable subject that can never be confused with an object."

4. This obvious point was not lost on the gospel writers who narrate the mocking words of the crowd with no small measure of irony: "Come down from the cross, if you are the Son of God!" (Matt. 27:40); "If you are the King of the Jews, save yourself!" (Luke 23:37); and, "Hail! King of the Jews" (John 19:3). That Jesus *didn't* call forth a legion of angels to deliver him from the agony of crucifixion or shoot laser beams from his eyes to melt off his tormentors' faces is the ultimate display of selflessness.

5. See John Dominic Crossan, *The Historical Jesus: The Life of a Mediterranean Jewish Peasant* (New York: HarperCollins, 1991) and John P. Meier, *A Marginal Jew: Rethinking the Historical Jesus*, vol. 1: *The Roots of the Problem and the Person* (New York: Doubleday, 1991).

6. Tony Jones, *Did God Kill Jesus? Searching for Love in History's Most Famous Execution* (New York: HarperOne, 2015), 270.

7. Karl Barth, *Epistle to the Romans*, trans. Edward C. Hoskyns (Oxford: Oxford University Press, 1968), 323: "To accompany [Jesus] along His road and become messengers on His behalf—that is to say, to allow the word of reconciliation to be spoken over them as a genuine condemnation against which they have no defense (1 Cor. v. 19, 20)—this is to love God."

8. See Jean-Luc Marion, *Reduction and Givenness: Investigations of Husserl, Heidegger, and Phenomenology* (Evanston, IL: Northwestern University Press, 1998), 203–4: "The more that that which or the one who reduces reduces

radically, the more things give themselves amply to it or him. But likewise, that which or the one who reduces lets itself or himself be measured by the dimension of what gives itself and be identified with and by the identity of that givenness in such a way that the amplitude of what gives (itself) always also anticipates the determination of that which or the one who reduces."

9. This image of paper cutting is from Ferdinand de Saussure, *Course in General Linguistics*, ed. Charles Bally, Albert Sechehaye and Albert Riedlinger, trans. Roy Harris (Chicago and La Salle, IL: Open Court, 1983), 111.

10. See Jean-Luc Marion, *The Erotic Phenomenon*, trans. Stephen E. Lewis (Chicago: University of Chicago Press), 70–71: "By admitting the possibility that this event issues from me in view of an other still undetermined—issues from me deep within an elsewhere that is more inward to me than me myself, preceded or validated by no assurance at all. In short, the point is to ask 'Can I love first?' rather than, 'Does anyone out there love me?'—which means, to behave like a lover who gives himself, rather than like one who is loved tit for tat."

11. I am indebted to Jacques Derrida's thinking in this regard. See Jacques Derrida, *Of Hospitality*, trans. John Bowlby (Stanford: Stanford University Press, 2000); idem, *The Gift of Death*, trans. David Wills (Chicago: University of Chicago Press, 1995 [1991]); and idem, *Adieu to Emmanuel Lévinas*, trans. Pascale-Anne Brault and Michael Naas (Stanford: Stanford University Press, 1999).

Chapter 9

1. Catherine Keller, *The Face of the Deep: A Theology of Becoming* (London: Routledge, 2003), 4.

2. Richard Kearney, *Anatheism: Returning to God After God* (New York: Columbia University Press, 2011), 170.

3. Jean-Louis Chrétien, *Under the Gaze of the Bible* (New York: Fordham University Press, 2014), 7.

4. Gustavo Gutiérrez, *Essential Writings*, ed. James B. Nickoloff (Maryknoll, NY: Orbis, 1996), 150: "The modes of God's presence determine the form of our encounter with God. If humanity, each person, is the living temple of God, we meet God in our encounter with others; we encounter God in the commitment to the historical becoming of humankind."

5. Sallie McFague, *Life Abundant (Searching for a New Framework)* (Minneapolis: Fortress Press, 2000), 136: "Since, for the Christian, God is always incarnate and present, there is no place on earth, no joy or wish that any creature experiences, no need or despair that they suffer, that is not a possible route to God."

6. Søren Kierkegaard, *Practice in Christianity*, ed. and trans. Howard V. Hong and Edna H. Hong (Princeton: Princeton University Press, 1991), 128.

7. Karl Barth, *Epistle to the Romans*, trans. Edward C. Hoskyns (Oxford: Oxford University Press, 1968), 69, 120–21.

8. Audre Lorde writes about our human propensity to ignore the other in terms of "human blindness," which she defines as "an inability to recognize the notion of difference as a dynamic human force, one which is enriching rather than threatening to the defined self." "Scratching the Surface: Some Notes on Barriers to Women and Loving," in *Sister Outsider: Essays and Speeches* (New York: Crossing, 2007), 45.

9. "Who is our neighbor: the Samaritan? the outcast? the enemy? Yes, yes, of course. But is it also the whale, the dolphin, and the rain forest. Our neighbor is the entire universe. We must love it as we love our self." Elizabeth A. Johnson, *Ask the Beasts: Darwin and the God of Love* (London: Bloomsbury, 2014), 281, citing Brian Patrick.

10. Gutiérrez, *Essential Writings*, 153: "The neighbor was the Samaritan who *approached* the wounded man and *made him his neighbor.* The neighbor, as has been said, is not the one whom I find in my path, but rather the one in whose path I place myself, the one whom I approach and actively seek."

11. See J. Cheryl Exum, "Ten Things Every Feminist Should Know About the Song of Songs," in *A Feminist Companion to the Song of Songs*, Second Series, ed. Athalya Brennar and Carole R. Fontaine (Sheffield: Sheffield Academic, 2000), 33. Exum rightly emphasizes the importance of an interpretive decision between the "voyeuristic gaze" that intrudes upon that which is seen and the "erotic gaze," which participates and preserves.

12. The sense of sight is the most common one mentioned in both theology and ethics; but those who commend alternative ways of knowing speak of sight in an alternative sense (i.e., Pseudo-Dionysius, Nicholas of Cusa, Meister Eckhart). Note that these are all dudes. See also Margaret A. Farley, *Personal Commitments: Beginning, Keeping, Changing* (San Francisco: Harper & Row, 1986), who writes that "artists, poets, saints—*learn to see* better and better. So, too, lovers who see what those who do not love cannot find, may learn to see better, to learn to see more" (54).

13. As James Cone puts it, "To ignore the historical context of the oppressed community and speak of God's politics in universal terms without specificity of words and deeds of the victims in struggle of freedom, is to distort the theological enterprise and the ethical dynamics of God's presence in the world 'to make and to keep human life human.'" *God of the Oppressed* (Maryknoll, NY: Orbis, 1997), 189.

14. See Teresa Okure, "First Was Life, Not the Book," in *To Cast Fire upon the Earth: Bible and Mission Collaborating in Today's Multicultural Global Context*, ed. Teresa Okure (Pietermaritzburg: Cluster, 2000), 194–214 and idem, "Reading from This Place: Some Prospects and Problems," in *Reading from This*

Place: Social Location and Biblical Interpretation, vol. 2, ed. Fernando F. Segovia and Mary Ann Tolbert (Minneapolis: Fortress Press, 1995), 55, 57.

15. See Gutiérrez, *Essential Writings*, 76.

16. Barth, *Epistle to the Romans*, 91: "Such realization and perception lie beyond the possibility of our knowledge, and are the becoming possible of that which is impossible."

Chapter 10

1. Audrey Lorde, "Uses of the Erotic: The Erotic as Power," in *Sister Outsider: Essays and Speeches* (New York: Crossing, 2007), 56.

2. "Not letting our beliefs and practices harden over into pure presence is a lot of what 'deconstruction' means." John D. Caputo, *Philosophy and Theology (Horizons in Theology)* (Nashville: Abingdon, 2006), 63.

3. See Jean-Luc Marion, *Being Given: Toward a Phenomenology of Givenness* (Stanford: Stanford University Press, 2003), 323.

4. Here I am deeply indebted to Jean-Luc Marion's reflections on what he labels "the saturated phenomenon." See Marion, *Being Given*, §§23–24; idem, "The Saturated Phenomenon," in *The Visible and the Revealed*, trans. Thomas A. Carlson (New York: Fordham University Press, 2008), 18–48; idem, "The Banality of Saturation," in *Counter-Experiences: Reading Jean-Luc Marion*, ed. Kevin Hart, trans. Jeffrey L. Kosky (Notre Dame: Notre Dame University Press, 2007), 383–418; and idem, *In Excess: Studies in the Saturated Phenomenon*, trans. Robyn Horner and Vincent Berrand (New York: Fordham University Press, 2002).

5. Stephen D. Moore, "Are There Impurities in the Living Water That the Johannine Jesus Dispenses?," *Biblical Interpretation* 1, no. 2 (1993): 85.

6. Barth was a prominent member of the Christian Social Party in Switzerland when he was a pastor. Later in life, Barth would write, "This Word concerns mankind in all times and places, the theologian in his own time and place, and the world in its occupation with the routine Problems of the everyday. This Word challenges the world in which X, Y, and Z appear—with their own big words—to have the say and to determine the lot of all men and things as well as the lot of theologians. While the theologian reads the newspaper, he cannot forget that he has just read Isaiah 40 or John 1 or Romans 8. *He*, at any rate, cannot suppress the knowledge that the Word of God speaks not only of an infinitely deeper need but also of an infinitely higher promise than the sum total of all the needs and promises characteristic of his time and place." Karl Barth, *Evangelical Theology: An Introduction*, trans. Foley Grover (Grand Rapids: Eerdmans, 1963), 78.

7. John D. Caputo, *What Would Jesus Deconstruct? The Good News of Postmodernism for the Church* (Grand Rapids: Baker Academic, 2007), 60–61: "Deconstruction is a way to dream, and dreaming is important, as Martin Luther King Junior made perfectly plain. The deconstruction is not only a dream and it is not only about the future. As a 'call' or solicitation, the event is no less a memory, a call back, a re-call to the past that has given us this name."

8. Mayra Rivera, *The Touch of Transcendence: A Postcolonial Theology of God* (Louisville: Westminster John Knox, 2007), 126.

Conclusion

1. Charles Taylor, *Sources of the Self: The Making of the Modern Identity* (Cambridge and New York: Cambridge University Press, 1989), 27.

2. Augustine, *On Christian Teaching*, trans. R. P. H. Green (Oxford and New York: Oxford University Press, 2008), 27.

3. Anselm, *Monologion*, in *Anselm of Canterbury: The Major Works*, ed. Brian Davies, trans. Simon Harrison (Oxford and New York: Oxford University Press, 1998), 79.